Silencing Gender, Age, Ethnicity and Cultural Biases in Leadership

Silencing Gender, Age, Ethnicity and Cultural Biases in Leadership

Edited by Camilla A. Montoya

Hamilton Books

Lanham • Boulder • New York • Toronto • London

Published by Hamilton Books
An imprint of The Rowman & Littlefield Publishing Group, Inc.
4501 Forbes Boulevard, Suite 200, Lanham, Maryland 20706
Hamilton Books Acquisitions Department (301) 459-3366

Unit A, Whitacre Mews, 26-34 Stannary Street, London SE11 4AB

Library of Congress Control Number: 2018953279
ISBN: 978-0-7618-7068-5 (pbk. : alk. paper)
ISBN: 978-0-7618-7069-2 (electronic)

♾️™ The paper used in this publication meets the minimum requirements of American
National Standard for Information Sciences Permanence of Paper for Printed Library
Materials, ANSI/NISO Z39.48-1992.

Printed in the United States of America

This book is dedicated to my dear husband, Jared Montoya, for always encouraging me in my endeavors, and keeping a positive "Why not? Let's do it!" attitude. I also thank my children, Lucas and Diego, for their love and support in everything I do, and my parents for the emphasis they have always placed on education.

In addition, I appreciate the push and motivation from my sister-in-law, Fawn-Amber Montoya, who helped me get this project off the ground, and I am equally grateful for the outstanding contribution from each author in the book.

Well, I know that the sun shines and fights for your day.
You hear it say, be strong, and let it go,
Just keep holding on,
Soon you'll see that you belong.

—Joshua Radin, "Belong"

Contents

Preface

"Shut up!" That is all I wanted to scream when I tried to infiltrate the group of men at the family party, who were discussing stories and accomplishments in their professional fields. I had the same career experience as they did, but I belonged in the kitchen with the other women, talking about recipes. I could not understand why my contributions to the first group were being dismissed; at work, I am respected amongst my peers, but when sharing time with family and friends, I found myself again and again being forced to join in the women's conversations about raising children, cooking tips, appliances, and the latest *novelas*. Even though I understood that for some of these women this lifestyle was a choice, it was not *my* choice.

Since I cannot possibly be the only woman in the United States to feel distressed about the impact of social biases placed on women, I decided to assemble a collection of true stories that can help others understand some of the challenges we face due to societal expectations. While compiling this work, I reached out to other amazing women from a variety of professional fields in leadership positions, all of whom were eager to share their experiences. However, I realized that our stories are more than just gender-related, and I thought it would be important to address the other social variables that make an impact on the career-versus-family dichotomy along with being female. Therefore, I was drawn to focus on ethnic minorities and on women of faith from diverse religious backgrounds at different stages of life.

Although anecdotal, the narrative in this book recounts real-life stories of Latinas in current or former leadership positions in the United States. The accounts are not to be interpreted as victimization of these minority women, but as statements of success despite adversities. In this title, "Silencing" takes on two meanings: The first, an adjective, suggesting that, as women and minorities, we have all once directly or indirectly been told that we should not be pursue careers, let alone leadership positions. The second meaning, a verb, denotes us, then, turning around and telling the world we can do it!

This text addresses the perspectives of eight Latinas in professional fields, and their experiences being silenced based on their age, gender, ethnicity and cultural biases in the United States. The authors, minority women, explore their observations of biases in their personal and professional lives, as they convey the individual stories of how their career goals may conflict with their culture's expectations for them. These chapters discuss the complexities of life choices for Latinas in workplace leadership, as they describe both the struggles of challenging social expectations, and their ability to balance their professional aspirations and cultural demands.

The book includes narratives of women both born in the United States, as well as others who were raised in Central and South America, and later immigrated to this country. This diversity in backgrounds allows the reader to understand not only the complex identities of what it means to be a Latina, but also the similarities in age and gender regardless of ethnicity. The authors address the intricacy of mixing their personal and professional world while offering recommendations for how to blend these two spaces.

These women's contributions should serve as a reminder and as encouragement to others in similar situations that, although difficult, they can attain professional growth and success while they also work through their cultural demands. So, when society is trying to quiet down our desire to contribute to the work that traditionally (White) men have accomplished, we can use these difficulties as growth opportunities, and empower ourselves to tell the world to hush in an attempt to bring an end to gender, age, ethnicity and cultural biases in leadership. As previously mentioned, the contributors of this book come from a variety of professional backgrounds, some heavily rooted in higher education, others in industry, while some have experience in both fields. They do share a communality, though, which is their heritage as Latinas in the United States.

The stories in this book are not atypical. Like the eight contributors, there are millions of other women who strive to balance their career and leadership aspirations against the social and cultural demands placed on them. This is not to say that professional accomplishments should be placed before personal or family well-being, but that all areas can be simultaneously and successfully managed. Unfortunately, the day when gender, age, ethnicity and cultural biases cease to exist is probably not coming as soon as we wish it would. However, it is important to stress that while, in some cases, the presence of such social expectations can further the gap between career and personal achievements, they should not impede women, minorities and people of faith in any stage of life to give up on their leadership potential.

Introduction

In the 20th century, there was an advancement in the focus given to global ideas in academic research. This phenomenon prompted numerous cross-cultural studies, starting in the 1960s and gaining strength in the 1990s.[1, 2] This integration of multiple cultures, merging together both in states of friction and collaboration, spurred the quest for understanding the relevance of cultural insight and its implications in the practice of leadership.[3, 4, 5] However, even though extensive work has been accomplished in exploring culture and promoting cultural intelligence at the national level, little cultural research exists from subcultural points of view.[6] Some examples of such subcultures are gender, age or generational, religious, and ethnic or regional groups, all of which are addressed in this book.

The global expansion of leadership includes a growing number of women and minorities seeking positions of power and authority. This increase requires a true understanding of the positive and negative roles that gender and other subcultural variables play in leadership, both in the present and future. While some national and religious cultures have been successful in closing the leadership gap for gender and other non-majority groups, other countries—including the United States—are far behind in securing similar results.[7, 8] Being that cross-cultural differences both at national levels and in subcultural clusters are an unmistakable reality in the 21st century workplace, leaders must learn to adapt and develop cultural intelligence in order to increase leadership effectiveness across cultural platforms.[9]

To frame the perspective of cultural demands and behavioral expectations in society through the lenses of a cultural leadership framework, it is important to point out that my native country of Brazil, along with most Latin American nations, ranks high in two dimensions of cultural theory: Uncertainty Avoidance—the way that societies deal with the unknown and the lack of structure—and Collectivism—the strength of human relationships and social connections—which are both revealed by high levels of emotional togetherness that Latin Americans generally display in their personal and professional lives. The Latin American cultural cluster also rates much higher than the United States regarding the dimension of Power Distance—or hierarchical inequality—which translates into Latino(a) subordinates not implementing a free-exchange style of communication with their leaders, resorting mostly to obeying orders. Contrary to what most might expect, though, Latin American scores on the Masculinity cultural dimension are lower than those of the United States'. However, social gender roles are still noticeably defined in Latin American culture, often detected in Latino men taking an assertive role, while women tend to be more caring and accepting of others. [10, 11, 12]

Further research findings regarding gender roles in Latin American cultures also indicate that, even though women make up close to a third of all heads of household in some countries—such as in Brazil—the overall culture advocates that it is more acceptable for women to reach their full potential in the family and home environment. Although their work is often not noticed, tradition imposes a gendered lifestyle where women's efforts should prevail in the domestic realm. Still, women in Latin American cultures frequently stand out and attain substantial influence in their communities through constant efforts toward community service and social causes. [13, 14, 15]

Even though the overall culture in the United States is more accepting of women in workplace leadership positions than in Latin American countries, and although women have found a sluggish improvement in the last few decades in how they are recognized in positions of authority, there is still a significant leadership opportunity gap between them and their male counterparts. It has been very common and socially acceptable for women to demonstrate leadership qualities in informal capacities, enhancing the lives of those they have served. However, most women have not had the same opportunity to achieve *formal* positions of leadership in this country. In order to increase the number of women in formal leadership roles, it is important to understand the circumstances and conditions that women face when placed in such positions of authority, including family needs and other expectations. [16, 17]

One such set of expectations is a person's religious affiliation and the accompanying social rules. Shaw states that "people from different cultures think in fundamentally different ways," [18] and included in this statement are cultural requirements imposed by religious beliefs. In the Christian faith— the theology to which most Latin Americans subscribe—devout members are expected to obey the cultural demand that they should submit themselves to their ecclesiastical leader, and irrefutably obey their words of guidance. Such practices have proven to be detrimental to women since most western religions and faith-based customs have been instituted following the rationale of their male founders. [19, 20] Some religions actually follow the egalitarian philosophy, teaching that men and women are to act and to be perceived as equals; however, this similarity in social status and power, typically only prevails in the home setting.[21, 22, 23]

Along with gender and religious biases, age discrimination is also a silencing threat in the workplace. With respect to age and generational issues, there seems to be more attention given to those on the older side of the spectrum, including the fact the United States federal law protects employees over the age of 40, but little consideration is given to worker prejudice when it happens due to his or her young age.[24] However, although younger employees can be seen as highly competent, they are also believed to have more control over their accomplishments. For this reason, supervisors typically blame the mistakes of younger workers on lack of effort instead of inability, which leads this generation of employees to receive more vigorous disciplining than their older peers. The younger workers also receive less training since there is a perception that they are skillful, but simply demonstrate low desire.[25]

In addition to the biases mentioned above, understanding regional subcultures is imperative because, although a geographical area can be situated in one particular nation, those living in these areas may adhere to differing social and cultural norms from those of the majority culture. For example, I will focus on the American side of the United States-Mexico border region since some of the contributors of this book come from this area. The mere fact that South Texas is located in the Unites States does not automatically mean that the cultural setting in the region matches the overall cultural scores Hofstede has identified for the United States.[26, 27] The population of South Texas is 81% Hispanic, and is most likely more similar to a Latin American cultural background than to the mainstream U.S. culture.[28, 29, 30] Therefore, it is predicted that in order to exercise effective leadership in South Texas (or other regional areas), a successful leader must understand the cultural differences between the region and the rest of the country in its entirety, as well as maintain awareness of the preferred leadership style associated with the cultural environment.

It is also worth mentioning that, although the concept of leading others is often associated with workplace settings, leadership can actually take place in several other contexts, both formal and informal, such as in the family, place of worship, community service groups, schools, and several others. The cultural adaptations required from leaders are ultimately a mechanism to achieve effectiveness. The concept of leadership effectiveness is, in other words, the capability leaders have of achieving positive results, which is an indispensable component of favorable transformation to any organization.[31] So, having flexibility in adjusting to different cultures and varied societal attitudes has increasingly become a mandatory trait for attaining success in global leadership.[32] Taking into consideration that 21st century societies are much more blended than ever before—bringing men and women, young and old, Latinos and Caucasians, Catholics and Muslims together—it is vital that we all learn to adapt and work together.

This book is divided into eight chapters, each written by a Latina in the United States. Some focus more on gender, others explore their specific cultural demands in depth, while others integrate several of the biases listed in the title. Each chapter focuses on turning a seemingly surely negative experience into a catalyst for personal and professional growth in leadership.

NOTES

1. Hofstede, G. (2006). What did GLOBE really measure? Researchers' minds versus respondents' minds. *Journal of International Business Studies, 37*(6), 882–896. doi:http://dx.doi.org/10.1057/palgrave.jibs.8400233

2. Hofstede, G. (2001). *Culture's consequences: comparing values, behaviors, institutions and organizations across nations* (2nd ed.). Thousand Oaks, Calif.: Sage.

3. Lonner, W. J. (2004). JCCP at 35: Commitment, continuity, and creative adaptation. *Journal of Cross-Cultural Psychology 35*(2). 123–136.

4. Mankowski, E. S., Galvez, G., and Glass, N. (2011). Interdisciplinary linkage of community psychology and cross-cultural psychology: History, values, and an illustrative research and action project on intimate partner violence. *American Journal of Community Psychology 47*(1/2). 127–143.

5. Kumar, R., Anjum, B., and Sinha, A. (2011). Cross-cultural interactions and leadership behaviour. *Researchers World: Journal of Arts, Science and Commerce 2*(3). 151–160.

6. Hofstede, G. (2001). *Culture's consequences: comparing values, behaviors, institutions and organizations across nations* (2nd ed.). Thousand Oaks, Calif.: Sage.

7. Kellerman, B. & Rhode, D. (Eds.). (2007). *Women and leadership: The state of play and strategies for change.* San Francisco, CA: Jossey-Bass.

8. Montoya, C. A. (2016). Overcoming impediments: The influence of culture and gender as obstacles and catalysts in leadership development. *Journal of Leadership and Management. 1*(7–8), 41–46.

9. Avolio, J., Walumbwa, F. O., & Weber, T. J. (2009). Leadership: Current theories, research, and future directions. *Annual Review of Psychology, 60*, 421–449. doi:10.1146/annurev.psych.60.110707.163621

10. Hofstede, G. H., Hofstede, G. J., & Minkov, M. (2010). *Cultures and organizations: Software of the mind: Intercultural cooperation and its importance for survival* (3rd ed.). New York: McGraw-Hill

11. Montoya, C. A., & Montoya, J. (2015). Cultural awareness in leadership strategy and marketing: Applying Hofstede's basic dilemmas to Brazil. *Journal of Leadership and Management. 1*(3), 13–20.

12. Hofstede, G. (2001). *Culture's consequences: comparing values, behaviors, institutions and organizations across nations* (2nd ed.). Thousand Oaks, Calif.: Sage.

13. Moraes, A., & Perkins, P. E. (2007). Women, equity and participatory water management in Brazil. *International Feminist Journal of Politics, 9*(4), 485–493. doi:10.1080/14616740701607986

14. Ramundo Staduto, J. A., Alves Nascimento, C., & de Souza, M. (2013). Ocupações e renda das mulheres e homens no rural do estado do Paraná, Brasil: Uma perspectiva de gênero. (Portuguese) [Occupations and earning of women and men in the rural areas in the state of Paraná, Brazil: A gender perspective.]. *Cuadernos De Desarrollo Rural, 10*(72), 91–115.

15. Montoya, C. A. (2016). Overcoming impediments: The influence of culture and gender as obstacles and catalysts in leadership development. *Journal of Leadership and Management. 1*(7-8), 41–46.

16. Kellerman, B. & Rhode, D. (Eds.). (2007). *Women and leadership: The state of play and strategies for change.* San Francisco, CA: Jossey-Bass.

17. Montoya, C. A. (2016). Overcoming impediments: The influence of culture and gender as obstacles and catalysts in leadership development. *Journal of Leadership and Management. 1*(7-8), 41–46.

18. Shaw, P. (2014). 'New treasures with the old': Addressing culture and gender imperialism in higher level theological education. *Evangelical Review of Theology, 38*(3), 265–279.

19. Shaw, P. (2014). 'New treasures with the old': Addressing culture and gender imperialism in higher level theological education. *Evangelical Review of Theology, 38*(3), 265–279.

20. Montoya, C. A. (2016). Overcoming impediments: The influence of culture and gender as obstacles and catalysts in leadership development. *Journal of Leadership and Management. 1*(7-8), 41–46.

21. The Church of Jesus Christ of Latter-day Saints. (1995). *The family: A proclamation to the world.* Retrieved from https://www.lds.org/bc/content/shared/content/english/pdf/language-materials/36035_eng.pdf?lang=eng

22. Fung, W. C. (2015). An interdependent view on women in leadership. *Asia Journal of Theology, 29*(1), 117–138.

23. Montoya, C. A. (2016). Overcoming impediments: The influence of culture and gender as obstacles and catalysts in leadership development. *Journal of Leadership and Management. 1*(7-8), 41–46.

24. Equal Employment Opportunity Commission (n.d.). *Age discrimination.* Washington, DC. Retrieved from https://www.eeoc.gov/laws/types/age.cfm.

25. Cox, C. B. (2010). *The role of age in causal attributions for poor performance: Target and rater effects.* Retrieved from ProQuest Digital Dissertations. (AAT 3421436)

26. Hofstede, G. (1980). *Culture's consequences: International differences in work-related values.* Beverly Hills, Calif.: Sage Publications.

27. Hofstede, G. (2001). *Culture's consequences: comparing values, behaviors, institutions and organizations across nations* (2nd ed.). Thousand Oaks, Calif.: Sage.

28. Combs, S. (2008). *Texas in focus.* Austin, Tex.: Texas Comptroller of Public Accounts, Research and Analysis Division. Retrieved from http://www.window.state.tx.us/specialrpt/tif/southtexas/pdf/SouthTexasFullReport.pdf

29. Hofstede, G. (1980). *Culture's consequences: International differences in work-related values.* Beverly Hills, Calif.: Sage Publications.

30. Hofstede, G. (2001). *Culture's consequences: comparing values, behaviors, institutions and organizations across nations* (2nd ed.). Thousand Oaks, Calif.: Sage.

31. Herbst, T. H., & Conradie, P. P. (2011). Leadership effectiveness in higher education: Managerial self-perceptions versus perceptions of others. *SAJIP: South African Journal of Industrial Psychology, 37*(1), 1–14. doi:10.4102/sajip.v37i1.867

32. Jayakumar, U. M. (2008). Can higher education meet the needs of an increasingly diverse and global society? Campus diversity and cross-cultural workforce competencies. *Harvard Educational Review, 78*(4), 615–651.

back to Florida for a full month. This time we were on our own, with no tour guides, no preset schedules, and no GPS technology. I spoke little conversational English, but could read it well. My three sisters were younger and did not have as much experience with the language, so it was mostly my duty to guide us around. This happened during my last semester of high school, and it was, in a way, a test to what was about to come in a few short months.

As a teenager, I spent my high school years telling my parents that as soon as I completed that phase of my life, I wanted to move over 6,000 miles away to attend college in the United States. My father did not want to let his oldest daughter move that far, and he would constantly warn me that living in the United States would not be anything like our Disneyworld experiences. He made sure to often point out that real life was no vacation and that I did not know anything about how life as a non-tourist in the United States would be. With much reluctance, my parents allowed me, their firstborn, a young 17-year-old Latina and family-oriented Christian, to leave everything I knew behind so I could act upon my ambitious dream of living in an unfamiliar land, master a new language, acculturate to a strange set of social expectations, and develop myself for future leadership opportunities.

As most idealistic teenagers, I did not quite grasp what challenges were still to come. Being accepted by my new peers in Utah was not difficult on a superficial level since as a White teenager of German and Swiss descent my physiognomy matched theirs. However, once my roommates and classmates started talking to me, they knew right away that I was not one of them. I had a strong accent, probably used words out of context, dressed somewhat differently from those around me, and—I can only imagine—made several culturally related "mistakes" without noticing that I was doing anything strange. And I realized, although as a stubborn teenager I refused to acknowledge, that my father was right all along: Living in mainstream America, was no visit to Disneyworld! I can say now that in those early years of living in the United States I was unable to make deep connections with average U.S. Americans, so I typically leaned on and associated with those who were more culturally similar to me due to their country of origin, or observance of Latin American customs.

Coming from a traditional family, I grew up in a home where my father worked as an engineer and provided financially for the household, while my mother cooked and tended to our day-to-day physical and emotional needs. My parents did not complain about the social expectations placed on them, and to this day they still quite enjoy their familial roles; however, abiding by such prescribed social and cultural norms was never as easy for me. Although I had always wanted to marry and raise children, I never felt that I could be personally fulfilled by these experiences alone. So, when I left the comfort of home and country to pursue an education in the United States, I knew I was preparing myself for a future that would neither match my mother's life course, nor her expectations for me.

This was particularly an even more strenuous decision because, in addition to Brazilian cultural influences, I was raised in a religious culture that promotes a patriarchal family structure and accompanying social roles. From the time I was 12 to 18 years old, I joined other young women in my congregation in reciting the Latter-day Saint (LDS) Young Women theme weekly in church youth class. The theme encouraged young girls to make an effort to focus our lives on attributes such as "faith, divine nature, individual worth, knowledge, choice and accountability, good works, integrity, and virtue."[1] Then, the theme added that as aimed to live according to these values, we would be ready to fortify our "home and family."[2] Although the core message in this saying is uplifting, and though LDS women are actually encouraged to earn an *education*, I knew that my decision to prepare myself to pursue a *career* in conjunction with motherhood could result in a cultural clash.

One instance of this conflict of attitudes occurred during my last semester in college, a private religious institution. It was Fall 1999, and I had just returned to Utah from a summer internship in Los Angeles, where my fiancé was living and working. During that summer, he proposed to me, and we set a wedding date for January 2000, which meant that we managed a long-distance and very short engagement relationship for one school semester, but this would allow me to complete my bachelor's degree before getting married. In my mind, there was no other way, and I was completely fine with it. We would make the Utah-California pilgrimage a few weekends during the semester, talk on the phone nightly, and write letters (yes, paper letters) for a few months, until I was finished with college and ready for the next stage of life.

That semester, I worked on campus as a teaching assistance for a professor of Portuguese, and one morning as I waited in a quiet classroom for students who rarely showed up for assistance, I made small talk with a male student in the hallway. He noticed my engagement ring, and our conversation became about my internship in California, my fiancé, our long-distance engagement, and marriage tips since this 20-something-year-old was married and full of advice. It was then that he decided that the few minutes we had spent together in the hallway were enough for him to share his strong impression that my life priorities were completely out of order. Grounded on his religious cultural biases, he did not hesitate to tell me that as a woman in the LDS faith, I should have known better, and that I should not have returned to Utah to finish my education since my fiancé was in a different state. In those few minutes, he proceeded to tell me that my first consideration should have been to get married, and then if ever possible contemplate finishing my coursework. I remember my disbelief that a man I had just met would dare to tell me that I should give up my academic achievements so that I could get married four or five months before my planned wedding date. It was as if he was trying to shut down any possibility of personal realization for me outside of family, marriage and motherhood.

Although I did not feel a similar sentiment from my professors and other university employees, in discussing this episode with my female peers, they shared many similar sexist experiences that seemed to stem from a commonplace mindset amongst the White American male students around us. What I could not comprehend was the contradiction between such stereotypical remarks and the refreshingly progressive message in Church leaders' counsel, including top leaders instructing women with messages such as "Each of you, single or married, regardless of age, has the opportunity to learn and to grow. Expand your knowledge, both intellectual and spiritual, to the full stature of your divine potential."[3] And if I was striving to excel in knowledge, which was after all one of the eight values in the LDS Young Women's theme, why was this guy now trying to tell me I should not do it in the name of womanhood? Why did this stranger even feel entitled to meddle in my life? This was no Disneyworld! I realized then that if I aspired to pursue a professional career and simultaneously build a family, I would have to confront this cultural dilemma which was imposed on me not only by my Latin American upbringing, but also by peer church members.

MARRIAGE AND FAMILY: STRUGGLES WITH PERSONAL GROWTH

A few weeks after completing my bachelor's degree, I got married. Graduating felt strange since it was December and the university did not offer commencement ceremonies at the end of Fall semester. I just kept having the odd sensation that I had stopped attending college because of my new relationship status. I had to constantly remind myself that I had indeed done all the work and earned my degree. Since we were in a transitional phase of our lives, my husband and I decided to leave for Brazil for approximately eight months while we waited to hear back from graduate programs for him and see where life would take us next.

Knowing that our stay in South America was temporary and that my husband did not at the time speak any Portuguese, we searched for English instruction jobs. We found a great school that connected us with mainly executives across the city of Sao Paulo, and we went all over the city, teaching students of all different levels of language proficiency on a part-time basis. We started with English only, but soon I also had students learning Spanish and French, as well as foreigners being tutored in Portuguese. This opportunity led me to develop a passion for teaching, but I also loved the lesson planning and the business side of the job. When we had been in Brazil for about four months, the school chose me amongst all teachers to develop an English consulting plan to teach telemarketers with zero foreign language experience how to pronounce the names of American and British music CDs and movies they were trying to sell over the phone. I was thriving in the organization and having a great time.

Having proven myself during those few months, the language school reached out to me and offered me a full-time mid-management position as a coordinator. They knew that we were only there in Brazil for a short amount of time, however they tried to persuade us to stay and establish our professional lives there. I was a young graduate at the time, and to me the possibilities were endless, but I was conscious of the fact that we had to return to the United States soon for my husband's graduate school work. By this time, he had already been accepted into a master's program and we had started planning our return to North America in the following months. I had to tell myself that this was just going to put a small hold on my career development, and that my primary obligation was going to be supporting my husband in his academic achievement. My national and religious upbringing had instilled in me that my role as a married woman was primarily to focus on family issues while my husband's was to prepare himself for professional development. While I stood behind this new adventure with the future in mind, it was with a heavy heart that we left Brazil in route to a new life back in the United States, where our lives would start over back in a strong religious environment.

Upon returning to the U.S., once again I went looking for a temporary position since this job was only supposed to last during my husband's graduate school years. I spent close to five years working for a company that I did not admire, in a professional role that promised no real growth. Since the position was not supposed to be long-term—and because I was a woman working in a patriarchal Christian society—I was never considered for leadership grooming while my male peers were being trained for advancement in the company. Often, the men with whom I worked were given new exciting projects with promising professional development opportunities while the female staff members in similar positions were assigned repetitive jobs. It was also common for our director to invite "the guys" to join him for lunch, networking outside the office and strengthening their bond, but the women were always left behind.

During this time, I also gave birth to both of our children, so I was juggling a husband in a highly demanding full-time master's and doctoral program, a toddler, a baby, and a full-time job. There was a period of time during those years when I would go to work at 5 a.m. so that I could be home by early afternoon. My husband would spend the mornings at home with our oldest (and at that time only) child, then we would have lunch together for 15 minutes, after which he would leave for school and work, and return after midnight. Because my job was supposed to be temporary and was meant to support our little family during the time my husband advanced in his education, I stuck with it for longer than I wish I had. However, while this experience might have held me behind professionally, it was still the right fit for our family circumstances since it offered flexible hours and allowed me to do "it all."

Soon after I returned to work following my second unpaid maternity leave, I chose to resign from this unsatisfying job and look for something that granted me more personal and professional fulfillment. In my search, I came across a part-time position at the state college nearby. I had always had a soft spot for higher education, and decided to give it a try even though I knew I would be earning less money by working fewer hours, but, one more time, this felt like the right move for our family. My husband was in the final stages of earning his Ph.D., we had two little boys to care for, and me spending more time at home would help satisfy their needs at that stage of life.

This was a perfect formula for the six months I worked at the college; while fulfilling the roles of wife and young mother, I was also very happy in my newfound position, and truly excited to grow in the institution. My bachelor's degree is in Visual Arts and Design with an emphasis in graphic design, and although my previous job was in graphic design, the environment was not creative and the work was mostly mechanic. This new job was different. I was working in the college's main marketing and creative services area, and all my coworkers exuded creativity. Looking back, I believe some of the best pieces in my design portfolio came from my experiences in that job.

Then, the time came. My husband completed his doctoral degree, and I was proud of him; however, his choice of pursuing a career in academia meant that we would need to pack up and move to whichever university offered him professorship. This happened at the same time that a full-time position became available for me in the job that I loved, but the unspoken agreement was, of course, that we would pack up our belongings and follow my husband's teaching opportunities since so much work had gone into preparing for it. The traditional Brazilian culture in which I was brought up, combined with the patriarchal expectations of my faith had both instilled in me, a woman, the duty to prioritize my husband's professional accomplishments before mine. So, struggling internally and resenting my husband despite my pride and excitement for his accomplishments, I felt like I was sacrificing my career and aspirations one more time for his professional benefit.

The dichotomy of my feelings could be summarized by the fact that within the first five years of my post-college professional experiences, I was offered promotions twice in jobs that I loved, and in organizations where I had the desire to develop my career. Both times, I had to pass up on the opportunities because my husband was first starting a doctoral degree, and then later finishing his Ph.D., so my responsibility was to move where he needed to move to study and then work. Nonetheless, from the perspective of the multiple cultural influences in my life, this was the proper decision for the family, so while we contemplated as a family if this move was the right direction for my husband's career, we did not explore the possibility of staying where we had been living for the potential benefit of *my* professional aspirations. Although this may come across as selfish and unfair, I must point out that our decision-making process had been impacted by the social expectations that had shaped both of our lives thus far; and, as a result, the choice to leave what we had behind for the advancement of my husband's career once again seemed natural. So, we packed our belongings and relocated 1,500 miles away to South Texas, a place where I felt I would need to start anew.

NEW LANDS: OPPOSITION OR OPPORTUNITY?

In addition to rethinking my professional course of action, I had to adjust to a new cultural setting as well. So far, my experience of living in the United States had been in a mainstream region of the country that followed typical American traditions. However, this new place felt different from what most would experience in average U.S. practices, which can be explained by staggering socioeconomic disparities, with an average per capita personal income rate approximately 42% lower in the Southern region of the state,[4] compared to the overall Texas average.[5] In addition to financial factors, the ethnic make-up of the population in South Texas is 81% Hispanic (White and non-White), and only 16.3% non-Hispanic Whites.[6] This means that the percentage of the Hispanic population in South Texas is more than double of the state's demographics—36%—and over five times the national data of 16%.[7]

Therefore, because the population of South Texas is predominantly Hispanic, it more closely matches the Latin American cultural cluster identification.[8, 9] This means that both employees and supervisors who relocate from other parts of the United States or from foreign countries to South Texas must learn to adapt to the cultural demands of the workplace in the region. To adjust, it is important to keep in mind that both the Latin American cultural orientation and the low socioeconomic background groups are more collectivistic and subscribe to higher levels of power distance.[10, 11] There is indication that certain workplace behavioral styles have a positive influence on interpersonal facilitation, job dedication and organizational support in individualistic cultures, whereas different combinations of professional conduct are better suited to promote effectiveness in collectivistic cultures, requiring workers to adapt their style to the expectation of the group.[12]

Because flexibility in adjusting to different cultures and societal attitudes has increasingly become a mandatory professional trait for attaining success in employment,[13] I knew that I would have to learn the required socio-professional cultural demands of this new place. And, even though I had grown up in Brazil, a Latin American country, my higher educational and professional experiences had mostly taken place in an Anglo-American socio-cultural setting, which left me somewhat unprepared for some of the experiences I encountered and had to handle in the years to come.

However, upon arrival in South Texas, I did not seek employment right away, but I first decided to try the stay-at-home motherhood route for a while, following a little closer to the cultural demands that had been embedded in me from a young age.[14] My religious background places significant stress on the importance of parenthood, teaching that the "family is central to the Creator's plan,"[15] and that fathers and mothers have the sacred responsibility to raise their children in virtue, ensuring to meet their temporal and "spiritual needs, and to teach them to love and serve one another, observe the commandments of God, and be law-abiding citizens."[16] Despite these cultural values and religious prescriptions, after a short period of three months at home, I craved the sense of empowerment, independence and personal development that comes from professional fulfillment, so I set out to break free from the religious norm previously placed on me.

This decision, however, did not come easily. I experienced real internal struggles knowing that looking for a new job meant that I would have to leave my one-year-old toddler in daycare for most of the day, recognizing that both my faith and my Brazilian background guided me to opt for a traditional route, and that my mother had chosen this customary path expecting that all four of her daughters, although educated, would make the same decision. Choosing to pursue personal and professional achievement seemed selfish now that my husband was working full time, and I did not *have to* work.

Therefore, in a true spirit of prayer and in keeping with my own core values, I sought spiritual guidance in determining what direction to take in life, and strongly felt that my family would benefit more emotionally, financially, and intellectually from me going back to the workplace than staying home. But, to make matters more difficult, once I made up my mind about going back to work, I found new opposition from some friends from my faith community. They were homemakers by choice, and one of whom did not hesitate to tell me that my place in society should not be in the workforce, and that it was my obligation in life to stay home with my children. Unfortunately, when we are not expecting to have certain conversations, the right responses only come to us in hindsight because there was a lot that I wish I had told her when she thought it was okay to confront me. "Shut up!" was definitely at the top of my list, after all, my decision of working or not-working outside the home was personal, and only my immediate family should have had a say in it. Therefore, I did not let this episode stop me, so I started my job search right away.

Providentially, the same week I began looking for employment, I found out that a graphic designer had just left his position at the university where my husband was now teaching. This was exciting because not only was the timing perfect, the opening was exactly in my area of expertise and in higher education again. I had a good feeling about this move, so I applied for the job and soon received a call for an on-campus interview. Even though this happened over a decade ago, I still vividly recall the setting. The gardens in the premises were well manicured, and the building, now occupied by university administrative offices, had been part of a historical fort that played an important role in the Mexican American War. As soon as I walked in, I introduced myself to the three people who were ready to interview me: The department's male director, the female assistant director, and a fellow male graphic designer, whom I shall call Eric.

The exchange seemed to go well, and everything felt right until the end of the interview, when I was instantly reminded that I was now in a Latin American cultural setting as the supervisor asked me what my plans were for childcare since I had a four-year-old son and a 13-month-old toddler. Although I knew the question was illegal and completely inappropriate, I was caught by surprise and simply responded that my husband and I would make the proper arrangements. A few years later, in retelling this occurrence to a female Caucasian supervisor, she told me that during her interview at the same institution, a highly-ranked male administrator asked her a similar question, while adding: "You do know this is a professional position, right?" Again, this was one of the constant reminders that even though our résumés were persuasive, the men in this society still viewed us primarily as caregivers.

Fortunately, the knowledge that I had young children at home, did not deter the director from hiring me, so, I accepted the job while keeping in mind my faith's counsel that "No other success can compensate for failure in the home."[17] These few words have served as a reminder throughout my career, helping me examine my life and prioritize my choices, making any necessary changes to ensure the existence of a healthy family unit. Once I started working, I came to realize that the university's culture was actually fairly family-friendly, which was another indicator to me that I had made the right decision.

This is not to say that everything was perfect and ran smoothly. There were questionable comments made to me that at that time I chose to classify simply as *interesting*. My then 43-year-old coworker Eric, the graphic designer who participated in my interview, told me that when he heard that a professor's wife was applying for the vacancy, his reaction was to question why an *old lady* would want to be a designer and how she would benefit the department. Eric was later relieved to find out that I was only 27 years old, which made a lot more sense to him. I left that conversation wondering why he would ever think that age had anything to do with creativity, work ethic, and productivity. I sarcastically told him that I was happy his worries were in vain.

This episode marked the first of many soon-to-come experiences that confirmed to me that a new job typically requires a need for adaptation and understanding of how the right combination of relationship- and task-oriented behaviors affects our duties and makes us more effective.[18, 19, 20] At the time that I started this new journey, I had a strong impression that there would be great opportunities for me to make a difference at the university. In the months to come, I was able to express my creativity through conceptual development and visual expression of several promotional design pieces. I can honestly say that I felt appreciated, and, for the first time in my professional life, I had a feeling that this would be a long-term journey.

Approximately one year later, my director was moved to a different division at the university, and his position became vacant. At that time, I often wondered if there was to be a search for a replacement, if I would ever qualify for his old job, and I concluded that at that time I felt unprepared for the task. For a number of months to follow, instead of reopening the unfilled director post, the decision was made to assign the office responsibilities to the assistant director, someone who was not fully trained for the job, displaying neither knowledge in our field of work, nor administrative skills. The issue with this appointment was that she was not prepared for the task of management, let alone leadership, so it created an obstacle for the team's advancement.

Regardless of the major challenges, this experience proved to be a pivotal lesson for me on the concepts of attitude and influence. Feeling uncared for after this supervisory transition, the four staff members in the office—including me—started using most of our time at work to complain about the lack of leadership we had been experiencing, and retelling stories of the assistant director's inability to get things done. In fact, we often had to tell our new boss when we needed to hold a staff meeting before she would schedule one, and, while at these meetings, we spent the majority of the time telling her what she needed to do next. The situation was becoming more and more distressing, and each day we had a larger number of stories to vent to each other.

However, one day I woke up and realized that I had become a part of the problem; that by complaining every day, and allowing others to do the same, I was contributing to the poisonous environment. I decided on that day that no matter how bad things were, or continued to be, I would not criticize her anymore, nor would I allow others to do so in my vicinity. At the same time, I decided that anything that needed to be done, I would take action and do it myself. From that point forward, a stunning transformation happened in the department. Slowly, everyone else stopped complaining, we all became much more productive than we had ever been, and we found contentment.

Addressing this exact type of transformation, Stephen Covey stated that reshaping our circumstances must initially take place intrinsically, beginning with the choices and attitudes of *one* individual.[21] It does not matter what position or title we hold, we can always be a catalyst of positive changes. After adjusting our own thoughts and actions first, and being mindful of our decision-making power, we gain the ability to influence others for the better. Often, we unknowingly *choose* to be victims of a bad situation by the way we react to our external circumstances, but as an alternative to this mindset, we must remember that if at any point in life we believe "the problem is *out there,* that very thought *is* the problem."[22] When we recognize that, as individuals, we have the ability to choose how to handle other people's damaging behavior, we gain the capacity to change our perspective, and to choose to make an impact in our immediate environment.

Acting on my new-found strength, in the years that followed, I volunteered for new projects every chance I got, I signed up for the university's human resources management trainings, and I accepted every challenge that came my way. Knowing that these opportunities were ultimately affording me professional growth through addressing challenges and gaining experience with every task I concluded, I was putting into practice Virgin Mobile USA's CEO Dan Schulman's metaphor that "no one can lift three hundred pounds unless they start much lower and work their way up."[23] During that time, not only did I learn the duties of my former director, but also acquired new skills that he did not previously have.

Around this time, the university hired an external candidate for a brand new Marketing and Communications associate vice president position, whom I will call Meagan. She brought in strong expertise in strategic decision making and departmental structuring, both of which we had been lacking. Her ideas were refreshing and invigorating, which not only kept the staff accountable and on course with our workload, but also inspired creativity as she involved us in several of the recommendations for change. One of the early issues another female coworker, whom I will call Daniela, and I pointed out to our new supervisor was the fact that there were three of us graphic designers doing the very same type of work, however, only our male peer designer, Eric, held the actual title of Graphic Designer. My position was classified as Computer Publishing Specialist II, and Daniela held a job title similar to mine, but at a lower level. There was an unspoken understanding that the three of us were ranked one above the other, as a traditional

stated that he had no intentions of following orders from a *woman* who had fewer years of professional experience than he did, let alone someone who was so much *younger* than him. He closed by saying that if I had any thoughts otherwise, that I was very wrong.[28] I. Was. Shocked.

Of course I had expected some level of interpersonal resistance to take place in addition to a mountain of setbacks in my new position, but I had not anticipated this level of direct hostility from someone who had been a friendly colleague for the past three and a half years. From an evolutionary perspective, it makes sense that underperforming males are threatened by female opponents,[29] but actually experiencing this attack took me by complete surprise. Was this an attempt to shut down any success I could achieve in the next few years? Was he expecting me to engage in a verbal war that would take us nowhere positive? Or was he simply trying to tell me to *shut up* and leave leadership to him, a member of the majority supervisory group: a middle-aged White man?

Even though the first few months ensuing my promotion were not easy, I avoided interpreting strained professional relationships as personal criticism, and I tried to be conscientious of taking measures to improve the atmosphere in our workplace. What followed can be explained by John W. Gardner, former United States Secretary of Health, Education, and Welfare, when he argued that the standard definition of leadership is superficial and inadequate, "so we cry out for leadership."[30] Sometimes people think it is easier to ignore the existence of problems around them if they do not believe they have the ability to solve these problems themselves. When confidence and motivation in people weaken, leaders encounter difficulty leading; however, effective leaders actually work to enhance these attributes in their employees.

Although this incident was definitely a trial I had not anticipated, I could not simply ignore it. This instance defined my ability to position myself as a constructive leader by giving me a chance to adapt, endure, and comprehend my surroundings from the get-go. It was now my turn to formulate my message in response to Eric's email. His remarks were loud and clear; he was disappointed and his pride was hurt. It was my choice now to press on his wound, or listen to what he was telling me between the lines and help us all grow from the experience. I chose to focus on the later, and responded by saying that I was sorry he felt the way he did, but it was imperative that we both found a way to continue working well together like we had in the previous years. I concluded my reply by letting him know that if he ever had a need to discuss strategies and ideas that would allow us to be a better department, that I was open to hearing what he had to say.

In spite of the fact that it was too soon to heal, Eric simply thanked me, and did just what he had just proclaimed he would never do: He listened back to what I had to say and followed my guidance in the months to follow. What I had been able to do was open a door where he felt welcomed to express his views and participate in making work-related suggestions. It is important for leaders to turn their subordinates into advisors. Even though many leaders today might see this council as a weakness by humanizing their interaction with their followers, a supportive interaction between leaders and followers can prove to be very effective to both parties. [31]

From that point on, throughout my career, I have been able to participate in different types of experiences with both my subordinates and my leaders; some of whom have been more open to personal interactions and vulnerability than others. Even though I have worked well under either style of leader, I have personally felt a stronger connection with those who have asked me questions and included me in the process of solving problems. I find that I was more willing to serve these leaders who saw me as an advisor and valued my opinion, versus those who have tried to accomplish everything on their own.

So, it was natural that now in a position of leadership, I would implement the same strategy I had benefitted from in the role of a follower. As a supervisor, I have also had the fortune of working with very talented people whose contributions have been indispensable to the positive achievements we were able to obtain. I have learned very much from my interactions with my subordinates, and they have reciprocated with willingness to go the extra mile for feeling included in the process. On the other hand, other employees of mine have not felt as comfortable sharing their opinions for different reasons. These employees were satisfied with quietly working from eight to five year after year, therefore my relationship with these workers was not as strong as with the ones previously mentioned. The exchange with the eight-to-fivers was very transactional and both parties have had to accept that this relationship is also acceptable.

Eric was one of these staff members. He came in on time, did his job, had little social interaction with other office members, and left promptly at five in the afternoon. For the most part, he just kept to himself and worked on his projects. However, about six months following my promotion, I needed to drive somewhere else in town for a work-related matter and Eric inquired if he could join me. I agreed, and, since our professional relationship had been strained, I assumed the car ride would be very awkward. We started out by making small talk and trying to focus mostly on task-oriented topics in order to keep the conversation centered around some sort of common ground. Once we had completed our errand, and started heading back to the office, the subject of the conversation shifted to a more personal angle. Out of nowhere, Eric asked me if I knew why he had requested to ride with me, and, at this point, I really had no indication of what he was getting at, so I just told him I had no idea. He proceeded to tell me that he spent a considerable amount of time thinking about what had taken place the last few months, and that he wanted to apologize for his behavior. I was extremely surprised!

Eric's comment in the car was pleasantly unexpected, and absolutely a testament to the efforts I had invested into trying to get all my staff to feel like they were part of a thriving team, that their voices were heard, and that they mattered as individuals. He continued on with the conversation, adding that, with the help of time and pondering, he understood now why Meagan had selected me for the leadership position, complimenting me on what I had been able to accomplish in a short period of time. I could attest now stronger than ever to Chinese philosopher Lao Tzu's principles as he shared that leaders must be selfless and unbiased, earning the trust of their followers through their servant actions.[32] And, ultimately, I felt a surge of humility as I accepted Eric's apology.

A few months following the car ride experience, a few members of our team attended an out-of-town conference, and while I flew from the airport closest to my house, Eric and Meagan flew on a different flight from a nearby airport. During a conference break, my boss said she had important information to share, and proceeded to tell me that during their plane trip, Eric acknowledged to her that he understood she had made the correct choice in turning him down for the promotion because he realized I was accomplishing more positive results than he ever would. Being aware of the emotional conflicts in our department, Meagan was shocked by his confession, and took the opportunity to congratulate me not only on my task-related success, but also my ability to cautiously handle the human aspect of the job. This experience was especially satisfying because Eric took the time to provide approving feedback about me to my superior only a few short months after having sent me a spiteful email.

Following this episode, the interpersonal atmosphere in our workplace improved. Eric, Daniela, and the other staff members were busy, productive, and creative. We had found our groove and had a good system going. We had learned to trust each other and became so unified that we would often finish each other's sentences. The spirit of collaboration was almost palpable. Soon, due to an organizational redesign, our departmental workload increased a great deal. We were all busier than ever, and somewhat touched by stress. I started working longer hours, getting back to my family later, and bringing work home with me. Shortly over a year following my promotion, I participated in an intensive, selective yearlong leadership program at the university during this time of turbulence in the political environment of the organization. Without noticing, I was not as cheerful anymore, but kept a good face in the office since I felt it was my duty to protect my staff from external hardships. Because of the difficult times, the constant fear of potential job loss, and the low morale issues across the institution, my employees started making more mistakes in their day-to-day jobs, and I found that I had become lenient with them to compensate for that over which we had no control.

Near the end of the leadership program, it occurred to me that in the previous months I had unwittingly been directing my frustrations toward my children. I had become harsh and impatient with them, usually *commanding* their next course of action—showering, brushing teeth, going to bed—without engaging them in the process. At that point, it dawned on me that I had been doing it all wrong; I was letting my staff get away with their frequent mistakes without fixing the problem at work, and, at the same time, I was being too tough on my children, who did not deserve such treatment from their mother. At this moment, I realized that although I had not caused my family any deep, permanent harm, I had forsaken my faith's council that "No other success can compensate for failure in the home,"[33] and it was only up to me to correct my mistakes.

Through this experience, I learned to recognize the distinction between family- and work-related requirements in a position of authority, and I learned a few valuable lessons when I realized that there was a big problem in my leadership: (a) I did not need to use the same leadership style both at work and at home, (b) employees and children alike must be empowered and engaged in what they do, (c) I still had a lot to learn about myself, and (d) I had to be willing to change myself first in order for my environment to improve. This new level of self-awareness provided me the ability to make the necessary adjustments, and my leadership influence enhanced both at work and at home.

This self-imposed exercise, in addition to the university's leadership program in which I was selected to participate, advanced my appreciation for leadership development. Therefore, in the following years, I continued to pursue opportunities to serve at the university, at home, and in the community. When the opportunity for me to start a master's program in Organizational Leadership presented itself, I eagerly accepted it, and fortunately I received much support from my husband, my children, my friends, my colleagues, and my supervisor. Ultimately, the combination of a displaying a positive outlook, employing strong organizational skills, demonstrating patience, taking time to listen to others, correcting mistakes, volunteering for new learning opportunities, and helping others develop themselves, culminated in me holding five different titles within eight years in the Marketing and Communications department at the university, the last one being Director of Marketing.

COMING HOME: TROUBLED CONNECTIONS

Despite this professional growth of which I was humbly proud, during the time I held a director title, I was spending Christmas with all my sisters, their husbands, my parents and other Brazilian friends, all of whom shared the same ethnic and religious background as mine. While the women were talking about the best pots and pans on the market, the most delicious cake recipes and innovative cooking tips, I felt more comfortable participating in the men's conversation regarding business and marketing. As I attempted to be a part of their group, not only were my comments mostly ignored, but I could feel that the small circle of my male relatives and friends was physically closing me out. At first, I thought it was a coincidence that they would position themselves one way or another, but after several attempts to join in, I confirmed that unconsciously they were shutting me up and kicking me out. I was the only woman attempting to take part in the conversation, and there was no place for me in the circle. I did not mention this to anyone at the party, but my husband, who is a feminist at heart, told me later that evening that he noticed the way the other men behaved and he was shocked and saddened by the situation.

This experience was an immediate reminder to me that both my Brazilian and religious cultures are much less open to women participating in business and leadership positions than the American culture that I had become accustomed to in South Texas, even though it is heavily influenced by Latin American traditions. It is true that people from diverse cultural backgrounds impose social norms fundamentally in a variety of different ways from one another, including those in regard to religious aspects. In Christian traditions, this also means that faithful followers comply with their leaders' teachings in order to be considered a devout member of the faith and a true believer. This reality applies mainly to female religious followers since most western religious practices came about through the work of men, following a male-dominant type of thought process.[34]

Although I consider myself to be devoted to my faith, my experience during Christmas at my sister's house made me realize that, even if unconsciously, the men present at the event believed that I was disregarding the doctrinal teaching that fathers and mothers have the sacred responsibility to raise their children in virtue, ensuring to meet their temporal and "spiritual needs, and to teach them to love and serve one another, observe the commandments of God, and be law-abiding citizens."[35] The council above, actually integrate two philosophies, egalitarian and interdependent, since men and women are regarded as having the same level of authority within the home, and since parents are instructed to display characteristics of service in the family.[36] Nevertheless, this suggested equal partnership traditionally only exists in the home setting of many faithful followers and does not extend to professional environments.[37] Therefore, in the way the men and women present at the holiday celebration understood the guidance above, it was solely my husband's duty to provide for our children's physical needs, while my responsibility was to dedicate my life only to instructing them in matters related to love and service. Thus, I belonged with the group on the other side of the room, discussing culinary achievements, cutlery, etiquette, or the ins and outs of fashion.

It was interesting for me to become aware at this point that having been removed from my native ethnic culture for so many years, in the act of trying to join the men in their conversation, I was neglecting the cultural demands that are placed on Brazilian women, especially those with a strong Christian background. I realized, then, that I had spent all my adult life challenging the cultural status quo in choosing to progress in my career and develop myself professionally instead of staying home and focusing on the needs of my children and spouse, housekeeping, and volunteering in the community while my husband alone provided for the family. [38]

EVOLVING FAMILY AND PERSONAL NEEDS: ADAPTATION

In spite of enjoying the company of my family, since I do not personally identify with the cultural norms placed on me to the extent that they all do, I was glad to return to work a few weeks later even though the workload was extremely demanding at that point. My position as director of marketing came in a time of once again intense institutional transitions as we were navigating the rough task of a merger with another nearby university. Some of the tasks involved sharing processes and ideas with our counterpart colleagues in an effort to come up with solutions for the new upcoming establishment of higher education. In addition, we participated in exercises associated with the selection of a new name, a successor mascot, and different university colors. While emotionally the sentiment at the organization was conflicting, bouncing back and forth from excitement to fear of change, the actual day-to-day labor was also arduous. There was a lot to be done in a short timeframe.

Following several months of working toward the partnership of the two higher education institutions, and after much deliberation, I decided to accept another job offer at the university. This new position would be considered a demotion and it came with a lower pay; however, it would grant me two paid months off each summer in exchange. As I analyzed all aspects of my life, 10 years after initially accepting work in South Texas, I realized that my priorities had shifted, and that it would be more beneficial for my overall health and life balance, as well as that of my family members, if I proceeded with this change in my career. Then, two years later, I altered my professional course again when I accepted a full-time lecturer position at the university, which has afforded me much joy and a great sense of accomplishment in the process of educating future leaders.

Throughout this journey, I have learned that adaptation is a key component of success. I look back and I think: "I did it! I changed myself, and I changed others around me." I broke the rules and, in the process, not only did I personally grow a great deal, but I also successfully groomed others on their own track to leadership development. I did it despite being Brazilian, and in spite of the path my cultural background suggested I should walk. I experienced Disneyworld, and I followed my dreams. Along the way, I encountered some who doubted my abilities in the workplace and tried to silence me. I just listened, and that changed everything.

NOTES

1. The Church of Jesus Christ of Latter-day Saints. (2009). *Young women personal progress.* Retrieved from https://www.lds.org/bc/content/shared/content/english/pdf/language-materials/36035_eng.pdf?lang=eng

2. The Church of Jesus Christ of Latter-day Saints. (2009). *Young women personal progress.* Retrieved from https://www.lds.org/bc/content/shared/content/english/pdf/language-materials/36035_eng.pdf?lang=eng

3. Monson, T. S. (1997). The mighty strength of the relief society. *Ensign.* Retrieved from https://www.lds.org/ensign/1997/11/the-mighty-strength-of-the-relief-society?lang=eng

4. Combs, S. (2008). *Texas in focus.* Austin, Tex.: Texas Comptroller of Public Accounts, Research and Analysis Division. Retrieved from http://www.window.state.tx.us/specialrpt/tif/southtexas/pdf/SouthTexasFullReport.pdf

5. U.S. Census Bureau (2005). *Household Income—Distribution by Income Level and State: 2005.* Washington, DC. Retrieved from http://www.census.gov/compendia/statab/tables/08s0684.xls.

6. Combs, S. (2008). *Texas in focus.* Austin, Tex.: Texas Comptroller of Public Accounts, Research and Analysis Division. Retrieved from http://www.window.state.tx.us/specialrpt/tif/southtexas/pdf/SouthTexasFullReport.pdf

7. U.S. Census Bureau (2010). *The Hispanic Population: 2010.* Washington, DC. Retrieved from http://www.census.gov/prod/cen2010/briefs/c2010br-04.pdf

8. Hofstede, G. (1980). *Culture's consequences: International differences in work-related values.* Beverly Hills, Calif.: Sage Publications.

9. Hofstede, G. (2001). *Culture's consequences: Comparing values, behaviors, institutions and organizations across nations* (2nd ed.). Thousand Oaks, Calif.: Sage.

10. Combs, S. (2008). *Texas in focus.* Austin, Tex.: Texas Comptroller of Public Accounts, Research and Analysis Division. Retrieved from http://www.window.state.tx.us/specialrpt/tif/southtexas/pdf/SouthTexasFullReport.pdf

11. Hofstede, G. (2001). *Culture's consequences: Comparing values, behaviors, institutions and organizations across nations* (2nd ed.). Thousand Oaks, Calif.: Sage.

12. Ersoy, N., Born, M., Derous, E., & Molen, H. T. (2012). The effect of cultural orientation and leadership style on self- versus other-oriented organizational citizenship behaviour in Turkey and the Netherlands. *Asian Journal of Social Psychology, 15*(4), 249-260. doi:10.1111/j.1467-839X.2012.01380.x

13. Jayakumar, U. M. (2008). Can higher education meet the needs of an increasingly diverse and global society? Campus diversity and cross-cultural workforce competencies. *Harvard Educational Review, 78*(4), 615–651.

14. Montoya, C. A. (2016). Overcoming impediments: The influence of culture and gender as obstacles and catalysts in leadership development. *Journal of Leadership and Management. 1*(7–8), 41–46.

15. The Church of Jesus Christ of Latter-day Saints. (1995). *The family: A proclamation to the world.* Retrieved from https://www.lds.org/bc/content/shared/content/english/pdf/language-materials/36035_eng.pdf?lang=eng

16. The Church of Jesus Christ of Latter-day Saints. (1995). *The family: A proclamation to the world.* Retrieved from https://www.lds.org/bc/content/shared/content/english/pdf/language-materials/36035_eng.pdf?lang=eng

17. McKay, D. O. (1964). First day morning meeting. *One Hundred Thirty-Fourth Annual Conference of The Church of Jesus Christ of Latter-day Saints.* 5. Retrieved from https://archive.org/stream/conferencereport1964a#page/n5/mode/2up/search/success

18. Stogdill, R. M. (1948). Personal factors associated with leadership: A survey of the literature. *Journal of Psychology, 25*, 35–71.

19. Northouse, P. (2013). *Leadership: Theory and practice* (6th ed.). Thousand Oaks, Calif.: Sage.

20. Hansson, P. H., & Andersen, J. A. (2007). The Swedish principal: Leadership style, decision- making style, and motivation profile. *International Journal of Leadership in Learning, 11*(8), 1–13.

21. Covey, S. R. (2004). *The 8th habit: From effectiveness to greatness.* New York, NY: Free Press.

22. Covey, S. R. (2004). *The 8th habit: From effectiveness to greatness.* New York, NY: Free Press.

23. George, B., & Sims, P. (2007). *True North: Discover your authentic leadership.* San Francisco, Calif.: Jossey-Bass.

24. Swim, J. K., & Cohen, L. L. (1997). Overt, covert, and subtle sexism: A comparison between the attitudes toward women and modern sexism scales. *Psychology of Women Quarterly, 21*, 103–118. doi:10.1111/j.1471-6402.1997.tb00103.x.

25. Travis, M. A. (2014). Disabling the gender pay gap: Lessons from the social model of disability. *Denver University Law Review, 91*(4), 893–923.

26. Drucker, P. F. (2010). Managing oneself. In J. T. McMahon (Ed.), *Leadership classics* (pp. 524–536). Long Grove, IL: Waveland Press, Inc.

27. Bennis, W. G., & Thomas, R. J. (2010). Crucibles of leadership. In J. T. McMahon (Ed.), *Leadership classics* (pp. 559–568). Long Grove, IL: Waveland Press, Inc.

28. Eric, personal communication, April 13, 2009.

29. Kasumovic, M. M., & Kuznekoff, J. H. (2015). Insights into sexism: Male status and performance moderates female-directed hostile and amicable behaviour. *Plos ONE, 10*(7), 1–14. doi:10.1371/journal.pone.0131613

30. Gardner, J. W. (1990). *On leadership.* New York, N.Y.: The Free Press.

31. George, B., & Sims, P. (2007). *True North: Discover your authentic leadership.* San Francisco, Calif.: Jossey-Bass.

32. Heider, J. (1986). The Tao of leadership: Lao Tzu's Tao Te Ching adapted for a new age. Atlanta, Ga.: Humanics New Age.

33. McKay, D. O. (1964). First day morning meeting. *One Hundred Thirty-Fourth Annual Conference of The Church of Jesus Christ of Latter-day Saints.* 5. Retrieved from https://archive.org/stream/conferencereport1964a#page/n5/mode/2up/search/success

34. Shaw, P. (2014). 'New treasures with the old': Addressing culture and gender imperialism in higher level theological education. *Evangelical Review of Theology, 38*(3), 265–279.

35. The Church of Jesus Christ of Latter-day Saints. (1995). *The family: A proclamation to the world.* Retrieved from https://www.lds.org/bc/content/shared/content/english/pdf/language-materials/36035_eng.pdf?lang=eng

36. Fung, W. C. (2015). An interdependent view on women in leadership. *Asia Journal of Theology, 29*(1), 117–138.

37. Montoya, C. A. (2016). Overcoming impediments: The influence of culture and gender as obstacles and catalysts in leadership development. *Journal of Leadership and Management. 1*(7–8), 41–46.

38. Montoya, C. A. (2016). Overcoming impediments: The influence of culture and gender as obstacles and catalysts in leadership development. *Journal of Leadership and Management. 1*(7–8), 41–46.

Chapter Two

How Professional Goals Conflict with Social Experiences for Gender, Age, Ethnicity and Culture

Julieta V. García

LA PROMESA

When my father was about eight years old, his family fled their home country to escape the turmoil and danger of the Mexican Revolution. As they crossed the border into the United States, their passport contained one photo of all six members of the family. I recall seeing the photo many years later and remembering how very sad and exiled they all looked.

My mother was born in the United States, a member of a pioneer family in deep South Texas. Her father owned a mercantile store in downtown Harlingen, but her family had to live on the "Mexican" side of town. Those families who lived in the small town who were also Mexican, could only swim in the public pool one day a year; the next day the pool was drained and cleaned.

My parents came of age during the Great Depression, a time when a college education was out of reach for most. And although both had excelled while in high school, my mother even being named salutatorian of her graduating class, neither was able to attend college. Their unfulfilled dreams for a college education fueled their desire to make sure that my brothers and I got ours. Every month, my parents placed five dollars into three college savings accounts designated for one purpose, and one purpose only—to fund our college education. It was not because my family had a lot of money—quite the contrary. My father's first job was as a janitor, but, eventually, he worked his way up to manage the same office where he had once emptied trash cans.

At the very young age of 40, our mother died of cancer. So, now alone, my father was left to raise my brothers and me. My oldest brother was 11, I was nine and our younger brother was six. One evening after my mother's death, I vividly remember our father sitting down at my mother's sewing machine. At first, he just stared at it. Then he called for me and asked that I help him thread the needle so that he could mend something. After our mother's death, jobs in our home were not gendered. We all took turns doing whatever task needed to be done. But, just as jobs at home had no gender; neither did expectations for doing well in school. My father expected for all three of us to go to college and excel. He would remind us of how smart our mother had been and how badly she had wanted to go to college. He would also remind us how badly he himself had wanted to go.

Growing up, I remember that we always seemed to be trying to get our father to use that college savings account money. Our house was small; it had only one bathroom and two small bedrooms. As the only woman in the household, I would beg him for another bathroom and ask if he would use some of our college savings to build it. He would respond, *"Ese dinero no se toca,"* or "That money cannot be touched." My brothers would ask him to buy a new car with that money; our cars were always five, six or seven years old by the time we got them. But he would not hear of it. His response was always the same, *"Ese dinero no se toca."* We never knew how much was in our savings accounts, or how much it cost to go to college, but what was crystal clear was that we were expected to attend college and do well once there.

At one point, my older brother, tired of school and of being under the watchful eye of my father, announced to us that he was leaving home and school to make his own way in the world. Defiantly, he asked my father for his portion of the college money that had been saved. Without hesitation nor apology, my father said, "That money is for college; if you don't use it to go to college yourself, then I will use it to go to college," so my brother decided to stay home and to return to school.

The savings account never amounted to the cost of sending three children to college, but it represented something more powerful than money; it came to symbolize a solemn *promesa* in our family that we would attend and do well in college. My brothers and I did all graduate from college. My father lived to see me named President of a community college on the border in deep South Texas. My older brother became a registered nurse who now owns a hospice business. My younger brother earned two degrees in engineering and, to this day, travels worldwide helping companies design new technology-based processes. Most of my cousins also graduated from college. In just one generation, education transformed our extended family that now includes lawyers, physicians, engineers, teachers, and me, the first Mexican-American woman appointed president of a college or university in the United

States. My family's story represents the power of a college education and the dedication and commitment of parents who hold high expectations for their children regardless of gender.

My father also lived long enough to get to know my children. My son and daughter have both graduated from college and have five children between them. My father would have adored his great-grandchildren; but I am convinced that even if they had asked him for money from those college savings accounts, he would have said the same thing to them, "*Ese dinero no se toca menos para el colegio.*"

For more than 20 years, I had the great privilege of leading the expansion of higher education opportunities in the border region that first welcomed my father's family to the United States. I have seen the difference a college education has made in individual families, and the powerful social impact it can have on the region. If in a democracy, the public—*not the rich, not the elite*, but the public—does not have access to high-quality public higher education, there will be no sustained democracy. But if there is, we fling open the doors of a college education to produce a new generation of voters, of Americans, of people proud of their destiny here in the United States, independent of their ethnic background. And if we do that well, these college graduates will be vested in our country, they will nurture it, they will protect it and they will sustain it. I cannot imagine any more important work to be involved in than sustaining the democracy of this wonderful country.

My life's work tried to represent my gift back to the sacred *promesa* with my parents. It has always been my hope that all children who grow up and lived in the Rio Grande Valley (RGV), in deep South Texas, have access to affordable high quality higher education. I have spent my career trying to make good on that *promesa*.

MARRIED TOO YOUNG

For a while there, I seemed to do everything wrong. I married much too young at the tender age of just 19, had two babies in quick succession; the first born the day after my 21st birthday and the second, just 13 months later. I had completed my first university degree, gotten admitted to graduate school at the University of Houston and had become best known for the fact that I seemed to always be pregnant. I recall someone referring to me as the pregnant Mexican lady. After completing my master's degree, my husband and I returned home to the RGV to raise our children in our hometown and to care for my father.

My first full-time teaching position was at the University of Texas–Pan American (UTPA) in Edinburg, Texas, a university about 60 miles west of Brownsville, my hometown. We lived in Brownsville, so early in the morning while my babies were still in bed, my mother-in-law would arrive at our home to care for them. Then, I would drive 60 miles to the university, spend the day teaching and then make the long trek home in the late afternoon. I hated spending two hours on the road daily and being so far from my children during the day. I also terribly disliked the culture of the university. It was in the early 1970s when the stigma of having a Spanish accent prevailed. In those days, UTPA required all students to pass a 'speech' test to graduate. Failing the speech test meant that you were required to take a class in Voice and Articulation, where you were taught to speak standard mid-American English. For short, I would call it "learning to speak like Walter Cronkite." As a member of the Speech Department, I was assigned the task of giving the students the speech test and then teaching the class to rid them of their Spanish accent. The majority of the students who "failed" the test were Latinos who had grown up learning English as a second language and still had remnants of their first language, or *accented* English.

My first run-in with the administration came when I flunked a student who was not Latino when he took the speech test. The student was a young man from East Texas who had a Texas drawl, sort of the way Governor Ann Richards spoke. I was told by the chairman of the department to change the grade and pass him; after all, the chairman explained, the student was not a Latino and the test was really meant only for those with Spanish-accented English. I refused. The entire speech test was demeaning and discriminated against the very students who I wanted to help. It was the first of many times that I would face losing my job to take an unpopular stand. I never sought confrontation, but it always seemed to find me.

Toward the end of that spring semester, I was offered a position teaching at the community college in Brownsville named Texas Southmost College (TSC), the college where I had begun my own higher education just six years earlier. It would require me to take a significant cut in pay and leave a more prestigious university faculty position to teach at a community college. But I would be close to my babies and I would not have to test students for their *accented* English. I resigned from UTPA and accepted the teaching position at TSC. The following day, the department chairman from UTPA called me furious that I was resigning. Even though I had caused him considerable heartburn, I was the only Latina in his department, and finding another Latina with a master's degree in Classical Rhetoric and Public Address was not going to be easy for him. The day I called to tell him that I was resigning, he told me that I was committing "professional suicide." I worried about that briefly, but not enough to turn down the new job offer. I believe that you should *never* hesitate to make a decision about your future if it places the needs of family first and allows you to maintain your integrity.

"YOU'RE LEAVING AGAIN?"

After teaching for two years at the community college and with my babies now a bit older, I decided to return to school to pursue my doctorate. I remember my father worrying that I would never settle down. *"Te vas de nuevo?"* or "You're leaving again?" He loved having me and my babies close to him. But both he and my mother had suffered from never having the opportunity to go to college themselves, and their unfilled dreams were now a real possibility for me. As much as he wanted us to stay home and be near him, I knew he was not going to stand in my way. To the contrary, he bought me a new Smith-Corona Selectric typewriter as a going away present and helped us pack our moving truck.

I received a Ford Foundation fellowship and talked my way into the doctoral program at the University of Texas at Austin (UT Austin). We packed up our babies, now three and four years old, and moved to married student housing. The plan was that I would complete my degree in just under three years so that we could then return home and have the babies begin first grade at home, and I could resume the care of my father. Family always came first.

UT Austin was a much friendlier place for me than the University of Houston had been. I was still the only Latina in the College of Communication, but the *ambiente* was quite distinctly different. It had been very competitive to get admitted into UT, but, once there, most folks seemed eager to help me succeed. One exception was a professor from whom I took a class that was required of all Communications majors. At the doctoral level, the classes were often quite small, only five to seven students in a class. That made it particularly difficult because you could not blend into the background; you were in deep competition with each other and there was no place to hide.

The class was taught by a fellow Latino, a rarity at UT Austin, who was a distinguished member of the faculty. This professor was a traditionalist and very conservative. I had been looking forward to taking his class partially because he was the only Latino on the faculty in the College of Communications. Besides, he carried the same last name as my father's. Somehow, I reasoned that he would probably be just a more educated version of many in my family, but I was wrong. It was a night class taught once a week. On any given night, it was his custom to question one student forcefully and mercilessly until the student literally crumbled and fell apart often leaving the classroom in tears. I had vowed that I would be the exception; that I would not let him get to me and that I would not be made to cry in class. After all, I reasoned, I was a grown woman, married with two children, I was not to be ridiculed.

My turn finally came. One night, he finally zeroed in on me; he began by unleashing a barrage of questions; I answered all I could. Then, he bore down deep enough into the subject at hand, that I could no longer answer. I froze knowing what was coming. Like a cobra readying for an attack, he slowly arched his back, took a deep breath and then unleashed a fresh new volley of questions. He was just getting started... This was the part he enjoyed the most, watching us squirm, humiliating us and then wiping the floor with whatever remnants we had left of our dignity.

I answered what I could. He maintained a relentless attack for what seemed like forever. But when the attack ended; it was a draw. I suppose I finally just tired him out. I never cried in the classroom, but as soon as class was over, I got into my old car to go home and see children, whom I had not seen all day, and to a husband, Oscar, who had not worn an ironed shirt since we had moved to Austin, and I cried. I do not remember driving home that night. When I arrived at the house, I found my babies already asleep and my husband waiting for me in our miniature living room. I unloaded on him recounting in excruciating detail and with a bit of melodrama, the events of the evening. He would later describe me as having "spewed like a volcano." I finished my tearful tirade by proclaiming that I wanted to leave UT, leave Austin, and return home.

Wisely, Oscar let a bit of silence fill the space as if to cool it down a bit. Then he spoke uncharacteristically slowly and calmly, "Then maybe he's right. Maybe you don't have what it takes to get the Ph.D. Maybe you simply aren't smart enough or capable enough. Because, if you're going to let what one man thinks determine what you do with your life, then maybe we made a mistake coming to UT." This was not what I expected. I wanted a Prince Charming to rise up, mount his white horse and slay the dragon for me. I naïvely believed that others could help me do what I could not do for myself. I had not yet grown my own courage. But what I was beginning to under-stand was much more powerful. Fortunately, I had married a man who knew that I had to grow my own strength and my own confidence; he believed in me and knew that the most important gift he could give me was to make sure that I believed in me, too. We finished the Ph.D. in record time and then returned home.

WAITING FOR THE PARADE

After spending three summers and four long semesters at UT, I completed my doctoral studies. I defended my dissertation in the summer of 1976, just in time for my son to begin first grade back home in Brownsville. We packed up another moving truck and returned home.

I had loved my time at UT. Not every day, of course, but most days. They were filled with stimulating conversations with other doctoral students, brilliant professors, learning and then practicing research methods. I had discovered that UT Austin had 22 libraries on campus and I was determined to visit each one. So, I did. I had several favorite ones where I would sit for hours on end reading and studying. Days in the library were my favorite. My last year at UT, I even had a carrel in the Tower. The iconic tower at UT holds stacks and stacks of books, each floor dedicated to a different subject. Doctoral students writing a dissertation were assigned a one-person size cubicle designed for individual study. Each cubicle could be locked so you could leave books and study material there overnight and each had a window overlooking the campus. I thought I had died and gone to heaven on the days that I spent in my personal carrel in the stacks of the Tower library.

Earlier, when I had been at the University of Houston, I never had time to study on campus. My babies were so very young, that I just drove to campus for my classes and then rushed home to care of them. At UT, I had placed the children in a Montessori school close to our apartment. The school would not allow the children to be picked up until after 3 p.m., after their naps and their snack. That meant that I had all day to teach, study and write. It was very important for me to be able to merge my academic interests as a student with the demands of my family as a wife and mother.

As importantly as what I learned from professors, was what I learned about myself at UT. I learned that, even though I was a Latina and was different from my peers, I could successfully compete with other very bright students. I had also learned that I could handle high levels of stress and navigate the political environment that exists just beneath the surface in most university departments.

After completing my doctoral studies, we returned to Brownsville and I returned to my teaching position at the community college. My UT professors were very disappointed that I was returning to the RGV in deep South Texas, and not allowing them to help me get a much better academic position on the national market. I did not understand then what I came to know much later, that the better placed their graduates were, the better they looked as well. There was no prestige to be gained from having one of their newly minted Ph.D.s go to a small community college on the U.S.-Mexico border. There were times when I questioned our decision to return home as well. In 1976, the year I graduated from UT Austin, only 1% of the doctorates nationwide were earned by Latinos. I was young, well credentialed, and Latina. All three would have been very advantageous on a national market, but we had always known that our place was back home, to raise our children close to their families and to help our community prosper.

I remember walking into the office of the Vice President of Academic Affairs (VPAA) when I returned to the college campus back in Brownsville.

I was so proud of my new degree and of the fact that it had taken me just two years and three summers to complete the degree. I announced to the VPAA that I had successfully defended my dissertation and that I was ready to return to teaching in the fall. He responded with a rather deadpan face, "That's good. Of course, I'll need verification that you've actually completed your doctorate before I can adjust your salary accordingly."

Secretly, I had expected a parade; not a real parade, of course, but I had expected that people would understand all that it had taken for us to move to Austin, to work so very hard for what I thought was a lifetime to complete the doctorate. I foolishly thought that at the very least, there would be a moment of congratulatory acclaim and recognition. Instead, I was merely admonished to not expect my salary to be adjusted until I produced proof of my new degree.

The fact is that there is no parade; never was or never will be. Not for most of us. What there is, is another job assignment, or another meal to be prepared, or another school event to attend for our children. The "parade" comes from within. It comes from you knowing what it took, what the competition looked like and felt like. It comes from newly acquired confidence that you have survived and thrived in the tall grass of high achieving individuals and that you will again.

RAISE YOUR HAND

When we are young students in the classroom, we raise our hands routinely when the teacher asks a question. Most of the time, we know the answer, but we raise it nonetheless to make sure we are noticed, we are viewed as smart, or simply because we know the answer. Typically, teachers tend to call on boys over girls; even though girls raise their hands more than often than boys.[1] So, at some point, we girls give up. We stop raising our hands. We answer only when asked, and then we answer demurely so that the boys will not think we are smarter than they are, or as not to appear to "show off," or so that we are not seen as complete nerds. By the time we are grown women, we may have stopped raising our hands completely for the reasons already stated, or just because we give up.

I was brought up with two brothers. One was a year and a half older than I was, and the other one about five years younger. There were no sisters, but there were plenty of *primas* (cousins). Perhaps it is cultural and the result of growing up in a matriarchal environment, or the result of growing up with boys, but either way, the fact is that I grew up with strong opinions and the ability to state them.

In elementary school, I won spelling bees and was always in competition for top grades with Les Hodgson, a good friend of mine. In junior high, I competed in the University Interscholastic League (UIL) poetry reading, declamation and the one-act play competitions. I was always placed in the "smart-kids" classroom. I was also a girl scout and was selected to be the troop leader. In high school, I tried out for cheerleading, but lost. So, I ran for class treasurer; I think I won. In college, I was in competitive debate. The rule was that if the debate team of two members was mixed—meaning it had one boy and one girl—the team had to debate in the Men's Division. As it turned out, my partner was a young man, so I debated in the Men's Division. I never shied away from competition, but I did not particularly like arguing and I never remember physically fighting another child. I could be mean, though, with a harsh word or a dirty look.

By the time I was in college trying to figure out what I wanted to study, I had ruled out anything in the medical field like being a speech therapist or a pharmacist. Both of those professions are noble, but they did not appeal to me at all. However, both had great appeal to my father. He was convinced that either one would be a perfect match for a young, smart woman, and he reasoned that the field of medicine is the most secure because people always find money when it comes to taking care of their health. He further thought that a job such as being a pharmacist was a mobile credential, and that for a young lady interested in also having a family, it was a perfect profession that would allow a woman to take time off to have a baby and then return to a secure job. I never said it to him, because he had always wanted to become a pharmacist himself, but I thought that being a pharmacist would be a very boring job. I could not see myself counting pills for the rest of my life. So, since I loved literature, reading, and the world of speech and communications, I majored in Speech and English. I had no idea what I would do with a degree in either, but I enjoyed the coursework and knew I would do well in it because I loved it so much. The ability to think on your feet, to make a compelling argument, to sell an idea and to persuade others of your ideas turned into a powerful instrument for me in my career.

My master's degree was in Classical Rhetoric and Public Address. I studied Cicero, Plato, Aristotle, and Descartes. I studied the use of logic and syllogistic reasoning, the use of ethos, pathos and logos when making a persuasive argument and the great speakers of American history. My doctoral studies were also in communications, but now with an emphasis in linguistics and the origin and evolution of the world's great languages. I was still not sure what I was going to do with my newfound expertise, but I loved studying so very much that I was confident it would take me somewhere good.

After I completed my doctoral studies, my husband and I returned home, and I returned to teaching at the community college. I was assigned to teach the exact same introductory speech communications courses that I had taught before earning my doctorate. I was completely disheartened. I do not know what I expected, but it was not to return to the same class assignment that I had taught with a master's degree. After all, I had become a different person after three years in doctoral studies at UT Austin. I thought about things I had never thought about before. I was complicated. I wanted to teach more, learn more and do research that was important. But why had I not thought about that before moving home? I knew that there was no university in our hometown. There was only a branch campus of a small university that had about 30 faculty and taught no more than 1,000 students. I had returned to be closer to my father and to raise my two babies now aged five and six, but what about everything else? I began to think that we had made a huge mistake in returning home. I was 27 years old, frustrated and angry, and very disappointed with where my life was headed. I could see myself morphing into an obnoxious, arrogant critic. I was always thinking, "I could organize that better..." or "What are they thinking? If I were in charge . . . !"

About that time, the president of the community college where I was teaching, Arnulfo Oliveira, was recruited to become the new president of the local university branch campus, Pan American University at Brownsville. There would be a search for a new president of the community college. So, I decided to apply; *I raised my hand.* I remember going home one day to tell my husband that I had decided to apply for the presidency. I also remember telling him that I was very unlikely to even get an interview. I was much too inexperienced, too young, and too much a Latina. I also told him that I *had to* apply; I had to signal that I could do more.

The snickering was palpable. I could almost hear it out loud as I walked down the hallways of the main classroom building coming from male and female faculty colleagues alike. "Who does she think she is?" seemed to be what they were all thinking. They, of course, were all veteran members of the faculty. But from among them, there were only two or three people at the college who had completed their doctorates. *But I had.* And I had graduated from arguably the best university in the state of Texas; and Texas is a big state. I never apologized for having achieved the doctorate.

As it turned out and against all odds, I was chosen by the board of trustees to be a finalist and to be interviewed. I was stunned; as was the broader college community, I am certain. My preparations began. Just like I had been accustomed to at UT, I began to study everything that I could get my hands on. I studied Texas higher education law, the various revenue streams available to community colleges in Texas and accrediting standards. I studied harder than I had when in my doctoral studies. All of a sudden, I felt like I was back in a new kind of debate competition: This time the winner would take all, the new job and the new presidency.

The interview was a sham. I should have known better, but I was young and very naïve. I was asked silly hypothetical questions like, "You have to go to a professional meeting; you must go with a man. Do you fly on the same plane? And once you get to your destination, do you stay at the same hotel?" Another trustee asked me, "How old are you?" This was asked although it was illegal to ask the question, and in spite of the fact that I had my birthday and birth year on my résumé.

I was not selected as the new president. But the new president, Albert Besteiro, who was astute enough to know that I should be kept busy or I was likely to cause him trouble, asked me to leave teaching and join the administration to chair the Self-Study Steering Committee for reaffirmation of accreditation with Southern Association of Colleges and Schools (SACS). I accepted the new assignment. I had no idea what SACS was or for that matter, what it really meant to seek reaffirmation of accreditation. But I had raised my hand to signal that I was interested in contributing more; I had no choice.

For the next three years, I learned more than I could have in a complete doctorate in higher education. I dare say, that I knew more than even a good president knows about accreditation and how the college measured up to the standards of accreditation. It was the best preparation I could have had when the opportunity to apply for the presidency, once again, surfaced about eight years later. But as importantly, I was back in learning mode. By the end of the self-study process, I knew how many cars the college owned and how much fuel they used. And more importantly, I also knew how many books we had in the library by subject area and which revenue streams paid for what operating expenses. I was back in "inspired and productive" mode and it felt wonderfully good.

After successfully gaining reaffirmation of accreditation for the college, I was invited to serve as Dean of Arts and Sciences. Following about five years in that position, the presidency opened up again. I raised my hand once more. This time I was selected, and I served as president of the community college for five years. When I was named president, I became the first Latina in the nation to be named president of a college. Girls need to raise their hands, whether they are in high school, college, or in life. We can compete, and quite often, we can do much better than the boys.

I WOULD DO IT ALL OVER AGAIN!

It has been my privilege to serve the people of the Rio Grande Valley, to help tell the myriad of powerful stories that each dream for themselves and for their families, to witness their struggles against great odds to earn a degree and launch a career, and to understand the vast potential of the people in South Texas that for too long were denied the opportunities that come from earning a college degree.

Chapter Three

Asserting the Power Within

Veronica Carrera

ESTABLISHING RESILIENCE

Being a Latina in the corporate world has allowed me to take advantage of some unique opportunities, break some barriers, and many times be the first to do something. When I first joined a large global financial institution almost 20 years ago, I started in an entry-level operations role where I got paid an entry-level salary. After a few months on the job, I noticed that there were things that my department could do much better. Therefore, I created a proposal to recommend a departmental restructuring. I showed it to the department manager and then to the Chief Operating Office (COO), who was next in command to the company's president. They eventually decided to implement my plan and the department was restructured according to my proposal. Around that time, I also requested to be the first to give a speech representing the accounting department in front of one of the toughest departments in the firm, Sales. The speech was so well received that after having been in the company for only less than a year, I was promoted to become a Regional Operations Manager.

This was only the beginning of a long, successful and challenging professional journey. Not long after, I crossed over to the organization's Terminal Division where I received great training on the financial markets. I received outstanding ratings as a sales person and eventually had the opportunity to become a manager in the Trading Solutions department, where I was the first Hispanic woman to become a leader in this area. After some time in this department, I finished my career in the organization on the Equity Trading floor. Again, I was the first Latina working in this group in the company's New York office.

Although this sounds like a common and natural career path, all this success did not come without challenges, push back, and tears. When I became a manager of the Trading Solutions division, I witnessed how almost any White man would easily get approved to get his MBA paid for by the company even though they were not in leadership positions, while I had to make a stronger effort, present my case, get denied, and try again. As I watched other ethnic minorities in the firm get denied financial support to advance their career, I knew that I could not give up trying. Eventually, I presented my case all the way up to a c-level executive at my company, who reviewed my many years of high performance, and, without hesitation, approved my request. This did not happen without some repercussions from middle- and upper-management as I went above them to state my case and ask for unbiased treatment. I know that I deserved those same opportunities even more so than others who had not achieved even close to the same level of performance that I had. I needed to learn to look at fear in the face and become fearless as I had to keep my eyes focused on the goal. I knew that I was not doing this only for myself, but also to open a way for others who look like me.

Even though it is a sad reality that people of color and other minorities have to try so much harder to get certain opportunities, it is important for us not to dwell on our disillusionment and resentment. While there are many out there who may question our capabilities because of our skin color, accent or place of origin, there are also some great leaders out there with an impeccable ethical and moral ground who want to see us succeed. They do not see us as "the others," but as their fellow colleagues, truly displaying a tangible humanity. Therefore, it is critical to not allow our judgement to stereotypically put everyone in a box. I have found it to be extremely important in my career development to keep my heart intact in spite of the many disappointments, and to not allow myself to crumble and dwell on bitterness in the face of injustice. Instead, it is my duty to fight for my rights so that the rights of others can be fought for as well, allowing them to rise with grace and strength. In my rise to leadership, I have learned to become a better human being who is capable of loving in the face of hate. I had to learn to be a woman who can hold onto hope even when my dreams seemed to be crushed by those who have not yet awakened to tolerance, pleading for compassion for myself and others like me.

THE EARLY JOURNEY

Prior to this pivotal experience in the world of finance, I had moved out of Utah after attending Brigham Young University (BYU), and had no corporate experience. My major at BYU was French literature, and since I was also pursuing a minor in Business, I had taken a few business courses. Therefore, before graduating with my bachelor's degree, I was fluent in French, in my mother tongue Spanish, and in English, while also managing to speak Portuguese fairly well. I have always loved to connect with people in meaningful ways, thus, learning languages became a way for me to connect with many others of different cultures and backgrounds.

My first job after school was as a flight attendant for one of the major airlines in the United States. Upon graduation, I could not decide what I wanted to do with my life, so I took this opportunity as a way to figure things out, but I knew that this was temporary. I spent a year working for the airline in order to have some fun exploring the world, and figuring out where I wanted to land long term. During this time, I traveled a lot to Paris, France, and I was one of the flight attendants who translated the announcements from English to French during the flight. Although I absolutely love French people and their culture, eventually I decided to develop my professional life, and chose New York City as my home base.

This shift began in 1999, when the job placement agency I was working with facilitated an interview with a prominent global financial institution, following some not very successful interviews with a couple of banks. Because the placement agents loved my background and personality, they were determined to get me into a great company. I showed up to the interview at this prominent global financial institution not understanding fully what the company did, but I was only going for an entry level position in the Accounting department and it helped that they needed a Portuguese speaker. The interview was supposed to take an hour, and, suddenly, I found myself talking to one person after the other and the interview process took over three hours. I was pleasantly surprised with everyone I met. I had never been afraid of public speaking, so I was able to connect well with each of the interviewers, and that day I must have interviewed with at least four people.

Within a couple of weeks, they invited me to come back for my final interview. One of the first questions I was asked by a high-level manager of that division was, "You came neck-to-neck with a candidate who has banking experience and speaks Portuguese perfectly as he is a native Brazilian. With this said, why should we hire *you*? You have no financial background; Portuguese is not your native language. So, why should we hire you?" I did not answer right away. There was just a comfortable silence after her question, but I looked at her right in the eyes, and, with the naïve confidence that I often carried with me as a young person, I said, "You can teach anyone about the financial markets, about this machine that is this company. You can teach anyone about the daily tasks to be performed here. But, you know what you can't teach?" Then I paused while she looked at me attentively, "You can't teach someone *passion, integrity, and great work ethic.* That is at the core of who I am. *That* you cannot teach anyone." I paused again and she looked at me attentively. Then, I proceeded, "I promise you that if you hire me, I am going to make you proud. You will hear about me for many years to come in this company." She kept her eyes locked on mine and then smiled. That same week I got a call from my agency that I was hired at the company. My first day was October 19, 1999.

A PATH OF GROWTH

This was the beginning of a wonderful and fruitful, but challenging career at this financial giant. As if it was a self-fulfilling prophecy, I ended up staying in this company for 17 years of my life. I moved up the ranks very quickly from one great opportunity to the next. My tenacity and insatiable hunger to learn and over-perform led me to pursue many challenging and, at times, unsurmountable opportunities, especially for a Latina like me. As my career progressed, I often found myself in spaces where my peers were mostly White, and, as I looked up the organizational structure, I noticed that the leadership just got Whiter and Whiter—and mostly made up of men.

Although I had started in the Accounting department, after only a few months, I transferred to Operations, and then to one the most sought out areas to work for, the Analytics and Financial Sales department, where only the best of the best are selected. I was often offered opportunities to transfer to some of the best areas of the firms. In retrospect, one reason for this growth was because I had the ability to communicate well in front of people in a creative, confident, and fun way despite English being my second language and me not culturally aligning with the majority of those around me. The more people who were present in the audience, the more thrilling it was for me. I was also very passionate about learning, and had a strong conviction of doing the right thing by our clients. This made me very visible within the firm and it caught the attention of upper management.

When I was still a new hire in the Accounting department, I became really interested in resolving a major structural and communicational issue that existed between my area and the Sales division. The two departments did not work well together; each area had very different organizational frameworks that were not aligned to service our customers effectively, including different incentives and goals. It was evident that this model was not sustainable in the long-term, and that this lack of congruency was affecting relationships with some of my company's biggest clients.

Consequently, while I was answering clients' questions over the phone about the issues they had with their corporate invoices, I was at the same time working on outlining the issues I thought the department had, and building a plan of action to resolve the issues. After a couple of months, I developed a proposal that I believed would solve these problems, and put it in front of senior management. I advised them to restructure the Accounting department to be aligned with the Sales division. One of the hardest things I had to do in this instance was to work from the perspective of their mindset.

Interestingly enough, even though most employees who worked in Operations made up a very diverse team, it was this group that I found the hardest to convince. Like most people, they did not like change and, therefore, I encountered a lot of resistance. But perhaps part of that resistance was due to this unspoken and subconscious cultural dynamic as they, too, felt that they were treated as "less than" or as "the others" by the Sales teams. The ones who were willing to listen to the new ideas I was introducing were the White women in senior management. As a woman of color, I would have expected support from my own people, but it was rather the people in management who are trained to be more open to change and process improvement who were willing to listen, to back me up and to execute. Also, to be frank, when it came to sharing my intellect and innovative disruptive ideas, back then, I never held a belief or thought that I was any different from others who came from dissimilar cultural backgrounds. In my mind, I was just as competent as my leaders were, and, wherever God had placed me, that is exactly where I belonged.

Therefore, I saw it as my duty to contribute to the improvement of my company, and I explained that we could not expect Sales to cater to Accounting as Sales is the revenue-generating engine of the company. Keeping the emphasis on the benefits for the organization, I made the argument that we needed to align ourselves—Accounting—with Sales because ultimately our goal was not only to decrease accounts receivables, but also to have a customer service-oriented mentality and help Sales sell more. Hence, I proposed to team up representatives in the Accounting department to a particular Sales region. This would allow them to work closely together and to get to know their customers intimately. After giving it some thought, senior management agreed that it was a fantastic idea, and, since it was my idea, I volunteered to give a presentation in front of all the Sales personnel.

The Accounting department had never had an employee present at the Sales meetings where hundreds of sales people gathered every Monday. They were seen as the toughest crowd at the firm. When I looked at this group in a conference room, it was mostly a sea of White people, so it was hard not to think that hardly anyone looked like me in this audience. However, I was extremely prepared, and my presentation was so successful that, that same day, a manager of another division walked to my floor to offer me a job as a Regional Operations manager. Eventually, the head of financial sales for all the Americas also approached me to join his team. This opportunity shifted the direction of my professional life as I was now going to learn in-depth information about the financial markets as well as all the different asset classes, and both my career and income potential could experience exponential growth.

Another reason for some of my success at the firm was due to my strong work ethic. Where I grew up in Ecuador, school was very rigorous. There was a culture of excellence that was instilled in all of us from a young age, ensuring that my friends and I were very dedicated to our work. I had to have incredible discipline to succeed as I was also an athlete and competed in pentathlons, nationally representing my school. My family was not tolerant of any grades lower than As, and I was expected to over perform. So, now as an adult, when I transferred to the financial markets sales area, barely knowing anything about stocks or bonds; I had no idea what was going to be required of me to learn. However, I worked hard through the training, especially since most people in my class already had a solid background of the topics being presented. While the majority of my colleagues worked until 6 p.m., I worked most days until 10 p.m., and was often the only person in the office that late. I did not want to feel like I was behind everyone else in possessing the knowledge that was required of me. I wanted to gain a deep understanding of the markets and the analysis of the different financial instruments: Stocks, bonds, options, futures, interest rate derivatives, commodities, mortgages, the economy, etc. I became fascinated with the information, and, in this role, I did not only have to learn the information in English, but also in Spanish, French and Portuguese. I was required to speak to clients all over the world, so I bought a finance dictionary to be able to translate the different data points, such as volatility, theta, delta, gamma, interest rate swap analysis, premiums, mortgage prepayment rates, bond pricing methodology, and others in different languages.

I remember one night I was staying late as usual. It must have been a little past 10 p.m. when I felt the presence of one of the security guards who often passed by to monitor the area. As he was walking by me, this was one of the first times I looked up, smiled and said hi. He smiled back, walked toward me and said, "Wow! I thought you were a very serious person... I was very intimidated to say hi to you." I think what he had noticed was my intensity as I tried to learn all these difficult concepts and I was too focused and very tired to be friendly. This time, we talked, and I was happy to learn that he was such a wonderful Puerto Rican guy. From that point on, he was the person who kept me company at the end of many late study nights in the office. How comforting it was to have conversations with someone who shared a similar cultural background; I felt like I had nothing to prove, and I felt at home in that space we shared in the workplace.

During this time of my career, I had wonderful managers in the Analytics department, perhaps even some of the finest. Later, when I transferred to Sales, I also had some very good leaders, but there were really bad ones, too. However, I was able to cope with the bad ones because of my strong professional performance in sales. I had built a wonderful reputation and a strong name for myself at the company. Most people in the New York office knew of me because of the many speaking presentations during the weekly Monday morning meetings, one of the biggest global events at the organization. My colleagues or managers often spoke of me as being very dynamic, passionate and a hard worker, as a true Latina. However, as I moved up in my career, I started to experience more resistance than support. I would hear comments from friends who overheard criticism of me, including a manager who once said while I was presenting, "I don't know who she thinks she is."

SPEAKING UP

This takes me to my next phase of my career; the stage when I realized that not everyone embraces you. There is no denying that moment when you come to the realization that you are different. That the illusion of equality or inclusion, accompanied by diversity trainings at a firm may be just a façade. Talks of acceptance sometimes are a way for some companies, not all, to brand themselves to the outside world. There came a point in my career that I had to stop and realize for myself that before I could continue believing any of these deceitfully and disingenuous messages of minority inclusion in the organizational hierarchy, I had to ask myself, "Who is at the top?" Seeing no one else who looked like me, I questioned the marketing implications and financial results of open-minded company positioning statements. Any powerful company can pay for great global rankings.

The challenge became more intense because, in my case, I sometimes did not know where the resistance came from. Was it because I was a woman? But there were quite a few White women doing fairly well even though I knew they had to prove themselves more than their male counterparts. Or was it because I was a darker Hispanic woman with an accent? Maybe it was because, on top of all these factors, I am also queer? The longer I stayed at the firm and the harder I tried to move up, the more I realized that it became more difficult for me to succeed due to the latter descriptions of who I am.

To illustrate this point, before I decided to do an Executive MBA at Cornell University, I would hear stories of several of my friends—who happen to be Black or Hispanic—about how they were denied tuition reimbursement to pursue their MBAs, and how they were full of disillusion, confusion and tears that came from this unfair treatment. I would also hear them say, "I have been here for over 10 years; I have given this company my all, and then some White guy hired within the last year and wanting to do an MBA, no questions are asked. He gets approved." One of my Black friends shared with me that when he confronted the head of Sales about the lack of support, the response he received from this supervisor was, "Why would you want to do an MBA? You don't need to do an MBA to succeed at this company!" I recall him telling me, "Well, if I don't need it, why is it okay for these newly hired White kids to receive tuition reimbursement for their MBA?! Why is an MBA okay for them, but not for me?"

Similarly, on another occasion, a Latina friend of mine, who had been at the firm for more than 10 years and was a manager in the Operations division at the time, told me that while other people received full tuition reimbursement of over $140 thousand, her manager had only approved about $15 thousand for her entire MBA program, and that was after a lot of resistance. Up to this point, all these stories I had heard were just tales that did not make sense to me. But then it came the day when I decided to pursue an Executive MBA program myself. Before I approached management for support, I proceeded to talk to a couple of White men in my department as they were pursuing their MBAs, inquiring about the application process and financial support. Both of them told me that the global manager was fully supportive, and that he signed the approval without any hesitation to get their MBA programs fully paid, at about $160 thousand each.

I was very excited and I was certain that everything would line up well for me as well. I had recently been promoted as a manager, and I was the first Latina female manager they had ever had in that division. So, I wrote an email expressing my interest in the program and explained how the MBA would prepare me to rise as a leader within the firm. A few minutes later, I received a response from the same global manager. "Veronica, I will be happy to talk about your plans. But I don't want to get your hopes high as we have never approved anyone for tuition reimbursement." I was stunned! I wondered if I had heard wrong from these other guys who were pursuing their graduate degrees. Without telling them anything about the email I had just received, I asked my coworkers again, "Hey, so I just want to confirm, did the global manager approve your MBA tuition or was it someone else?" Their answer left me speechless, "Yeah, he did. You should have no problems. It was a quick process."

I hurt. I hurt because of the lies of a leader I was supposed to trust and continue to work for. I was in shock, and I felt as if I was outside of my body. At this point, I was no longer experiencing somebody else's story; it was now *my* story. At that moment, I did not feel capable of confronting the situation and all I could do was stare at my boss' email. Even though I had been treated differently in the past for being different, discrimination had never become more tangible in the workplace. I started to question myself as a likable and capable human being. At that moment, the only way that I was able to cope with it was to stay silent; that silence that makes you feel like a coward for not speaking up. The feeling of hopelessness, mistrust and despair had now entered my being. Can you tell your boss he is a liar? A racist? A phony? No, you can't, but there is something volcanic inside of your soul that wishes you could. Those in power can silence you in ways that you start feeling powerless and belittled.

This took me back to my first day in college in Idaho. I went there for one semester to finish a couple of courses before I transferred to BYU. All that was required for me to finish was an English class with at least a B grade before I could transfer out. When I arrived at the administrative office, the assistant told me that the class was full, but, that since this is a required course for me to transfer, the professor was obliged to let me in. She suggested I go to his office right away. I walked in and saw this older White man in his late 50s sitting on a black leather chair behind his desk. I was so happy to be going to college there that I greeted him cheerfully, "Professor, my name is Veronica Carrera and I am here just for one semester, just to complete required courses, and then transfer to BYU in Provo, Utah. But I need to take your class and I need your approval to get in." He looked at me and started to smile and gave a quick laugh. I laughed with him as well since I thought he was just happy to meet me. Then, he started to speak, "You, Spanish people! You think you can come here and compete with the Americans, you will be lucky if you get a D in my class." During classes, I would raise my hand to participate and he completely ignored me all semester. I worked very hard throughout the whole semester so that I could prove this professor wrong. I got a tutor, I worked diligently in my assignments and I ended up getting an A–in his class.

I was not raised to stay silent, to act like a victim. So, now facing injustice in my company, soon after this incident with my boss, I decided to have a face-to-face follow up discussion with the same leader and the Chief Operating Officer, a close friend of his whom he had recently hired. The meeting ended up nowhere. With a poker face, they gave me the same answer and told me that they knew of no one whom the company had sponsored in this division, including himself, that he did not get any tuition assistance from the organization when he attended graduate school. I had been told otherwise by others who knew him well.

Although I understand it is a privilege and not an obligation for a company to sponsor any of its employees to obtain a higher degree, it is not a privilege reserved only for those who look like the people at the top. In this case, White men and women who, in some cases had only been with the firm a year or so or who did not hold a management role, were given the tuition benefit without any hesitation or reservations; it was just *their* privilege. During this time, I reflected on so many of my Latino or Black friends' stories, and the answers they had received echoed in my mind, "Why would you want to do an MBA? *You* do not need one."

I told myself that even though I had not understood my friends' disillusionment, pain and disappointment until it affected me, I was not going to just sit still and give up. I was going to do it for myself and for others, so I requested a meeting with a c-level executive at the firm and expressed my concerns. I recollect starting my conversation this way, "Thank you for being so kind to give me this time. I came here because I don't believe as a firm this is what the organization stands for. I believe you want the company to stand by its values and the integrity of its mission. I am a star employee; I challenge you to check my records. I have even been ranked on the top 1% in the Sales division, and I am now a manager. In spite of all of this, I have been told that the company cannot sponsor me for my education and I am not the only one. Every year, the institution sponsors three people in Ivy League universities. We have more people of color being accepted at these universities, and I know there are minorities in this company who were denied tuition assistance while White people were approved for full tuition reimbursement. What if the universities start realizing that this is a trend for this respected corporation? Is this the reputation you want for the firm?" I expressed my disappointment on behalf of my people, and I paused as I contained my tears. This c-level executive listened to me attentively and then told me that Human Resources would run an investigation. Two weeks later, I was called back to this leader's office, and I am not sure what she found out through this investigation, but she said, "I want to apologize on behalf of these men; I am not sure why they are like this." I felt her sincerity and I even think her eyes were a bit emotional. By the time I got back to my desk, I had received an email stating that my Executive MBA tuition for Cornell University had been fully approved.

This was not the only issue I reported, though. During this time, I had also publicly come out as gay at the firm. Once I confided in some people in the LGBT community at the organization, they asked me if I could be part of a company video. I thought about it for some time; I was scared, but I moved forward with it. Everyone knew me as a Mormon since I had grown up as one. Even though I had recently stopped attending the Mormon church, no one really knew I had left as I kept the same standards, not drinking or smoking, along with keeping a lot of strict rules for my life. I was terrified of now being found out; being known as a Mormon for many years and suddenly coming out as queer. After the recording, I thought about going back and asking them to cut me out of the whole production, but then I told myself, "It is done!" Also, I was asked by the CEO during a private dinner with me and a few others queer employees how he could advance the LGBT agenda as his own brother was gay. He did express that he felt the company was doing a lot by giving health benefits to the partners of LGBT employees. I remember being the one telling him that he needed to publicly acknowledge that as the CEO of the company, he stood by the LGBT community. I even shared a Ginette Sagan quote with him, stating that "Silence in the face of injustice is complicity with the oppressor."[1] He did agree and, in less than a month, there was a worldwide email sent from him to the entire organization, acknowledging his support for LGBT employees.

The video came out and it was shown to employees worldwide. Suddenly, I had a few warm emails in my inbox congratulating me for my courage. Nevertheless, I now had to walk around the firm feeling naked while functioning within this new paradigm of who or what I was now supposed to be. I was a manager at that time and I had warned the CEO of that division via email that this video was going to be released, and that since I was a manager that I wanted to make sure people were comfortable with this new development. His reply was short, professional and supportive. My global manager reported to him and since there is a comradeship among most leaders who are on top, I thought they must all be on board.

In spite of telling myself that everything would be okay, and that there was nothing to panic about, that things would just go back to normal, I started to feel a change in the attitudes and behaviors from my direct managers, particularly this global leader. They worked very closely with this unkind, rather mean, Human Resources representative who acted as their sniper. Suddenly, they all started to question everything I did. I remember on one occurrence, they wanted me to document any evidence that would help me get one of my employees fired. I was trying to make a case that she should not get fired as she was doing everything she could to improve. I had to turn in a three-page document on an ongoing basis to report her progress. One week, I submitted the report to Human Resources, and a day later I saw my office phone ringing; it was the Human Resources representative. With a cold and miserable voice, she said, "We need you to come to the conference room now."

My intuition did not fail me this time. Before I went, I printed the form I had sent her the previous day and put it in my pocket. As soon as I approached the conference room, which was all covered by glass, I could see that my direct manager, my global manager and the Human Resources representative were all inside. When I walked in, all eyes were on me, and I did not sit down. The Human Resources representative began to talk, saying "There is a concern that you are not following procedure and not turning in the information that we have requested from you for this employee." She stopped, and, standing in a corner, I asked, "What are you referring to?" She interrupted with a harsh voice, "You are supposed to turn in three pages with a report of what this employee has done or not done." Surprisingly, I kept calm, "Show me what you are talking about," I said as I looked at her directly in the eyes. She brought up her file on the company's terminal, with only two pages out of the three pages uploaded. She then proceeded to speak rudely as she raised her voice to tell me that I had failed to follow my duties as a manager. I let her finish—the other managers were silent just looking at me emotionlessly—I could have been in an interrogation room and it would not

During the last semester of the MBA program, my team and I had to work as consultants for an American company and fly to China as part of a final project to analyze our assigned company's business in that area. I spent most of my time in Beijing, interviewing their customers, analyzing their competitors, and when I got to the hotel at night, I took time to take a Series 7 practice test. I barely got to see a couple of historical sites like the Great Wall of China and the Forbidden City. When I got to Shanghai, a place I absolutely adored, my team asked me to write another report while they interviewed some employees. Since I was only there for a day, I rushed to walk around the area for a few hours so that I can get back to the hotel and finish the assignment.

A week after my return to the United States, I took the Series 7 on a Monday, and I passed it. That same weekend, I graduated from my MBA program at Cornell. I could not believe I was able to do it all! I still remember my eyes filled with tears; it was truly one of the best weeks of my life. A few months after graduating, I received an email from the Assistant Dean at Cornell telling me that they had nominated me as the best MBA for class for 2015. Each top MBA school had to submit their nominee to a ranking agency, Poets & Quants. I was asked to submit my story and answer a few meaningful questions, and, within weeks, I saw my name being announced on social media: "Poets & Quants selects Veronica Carrera, Cornell MBA, as the top MBA of 2015." What a joy I felt and, interestingly enough, I also thought, "Am I *that* person? Am I good enough to be nominated as the *best* MBA?" But regardless of that impostor syndrome that sometimes enters our minds, with the help of loving friends, I had to affirm to myself, "Yes, I *am* deserving of this." That same week, the c-level executive who had approved my Executive MBA sent me a loving note that said, "Your mom, who is watching from heaven, must be so proud!"

Following this, I started to work in the Equity Trading Floor as a junior trader. My particular team was made up entirely of White men who had traded most of their lives. I heard from my manager, who was a White woman and one of my biggest supporters, that there was resistance from some of these men about hiring me. She stated that they were concerned I had not traded before and they were not sure that I would be a fit in that role. I believe she made a case stating that I had a good reputation in the company and that I was finishing an MBA from Cornell, and that she did not see a problem with me learning how to trade. At the end, it was her decision, and I was hired. I will always be deeply grateful to her as she was my pillar and greatest support when I started in this team. The men were polite, respectful, but not very open to help me learn. I had to pull teeth to get them to train me in their craft. But, little by little, I was able to identify some of the things that I should learn first so that I could be helpful to them. I made sure to learn how to put together some client reports with exactitude, and, because of this,

I had the men in this team start reaching out to me for help. They started to trust me and ask me to put in some trades for them and create their clients' reports, which I happily did. I was excited to know that I was able to do something to help and to start sensing their approval.

During this time, a White woman was transferred from the San Francisco office to the New York headquarters. She was helpful, but at the same time, I did not feel her sincerity in our professional relationship. She sat on the same row as me and she was also an experienced trader; however, she was still relatively new to the organization and struggled with some functionality. She saw how the guys would walk to my desk and ask me to enter some trades for them or create a report. This led her to made a highly offensive comment about me, stating "Even a monkey can learn my job." At first, I felt as if someone had punched me in the stomach. I asked myself, "Is this an American expression? Perhaps, I am misinterpreting what she is trying to say." On another occasion, she repeated it in front of my boss as she explained how I was learning a lot, "Even a monkey can learn my job." I was appalled. My boss remained quiet... I do not even know if she knew what to say in that moment. Then, on another occasion, she said it a third time when referring to me, "Even a monkey can learn my job." I, then, became visibly upset. I looked at her and said, "This is no longer okay!" She never repeated it again after that. But I sure thought about it a few times after that. There was another young White man hired to perform some similar duties as mine, and I never heard her say that to him. Why then was it okay to say it to me?

When faced with such open instances of prejudice, I think that in one's mind, one does not know what to think, what to feel in the moment, so one can start to feel just pure resentment. But as I learned with time to stand up for myself in a strong, assertive and compassionate way, I started to have more inner peace. I learned to let go and forgive the ignorant violent words and behavior from those who have not yet awakened. Those souls who have the sick illusion that somehow, because of where they are from, they are any better than the rest of us. There is work to be done so this type of violence does not continue. We are all responsible to bring justice and fairness in the workplace and in the world. Whether one is White, Native American, Black, Latinx, Asian, we all have a history to atone for, and a unique opportunity in this generation to heal the world.

TRIUMPH

Seeking something different in my life, after 17 years at this company, I decided to leave the firm. I had to do a lot of internal work to forgive, to move on and to take only the good that this organization has given me. There was a lot of good. A lot of wonderful stories and friendships that I made, and that I will never forget. It has a process for me to learn how to deal with the bad, how to never be silenced again, how to speak up and claim my dignity so that I can love and forgive. As I said goodbye, many who knew me sent me some beautiful notes and almost everyone said they would never forget my honesty, my integrity, my heart, but most of all how much they would miss me at every company party because I danced like no one was watching, and that I was truly the life of every party! My prayer to all, then, is, "May we continue to dance with compassion, determination, and love in this journey of life."

NOTE

1. Amnesty International (n.d.). *The Ginetta Sagan award.* Retrieved from https://www.amnestyusa.org/about-us/grants-and-awards/ginetta-sagan-award/

Chapter Four

No Laughing Matter

Gender Stereotypes in the Workplace

Isis Lopez

HOW IT ALL STARTED: DEFINING HAIR

I have had what is considered long hair most of my life—below the shoulder but above my hips. From a very young age, my mother discouraged my sister and I from cutting it any shorter than shoulder length. She argued that long hair accentuated our femininity as women and made us look beautiful, and we must take full advantage of our beauty and youth. When I turned 14 years old, I was due for a trim. Because we kept our hair long, we only trimmed it once or twice a year to cut off any damage or split ends. As the usual trim routine worked out, I asked my mother to drop me off at the beauty salon to get a hair trim before the start of the school year. My mother agreed to drop me off and pick me up once I was done.

The lady who did my hair at the time rented a small corner in a little quaint beauty salon full of pictures of hair models from the 1980s, with large puffed out hair and neon makeup. The pictures had a glowing effect on them. The worn down wooden floor would creek on any heavy step, and the smell of ammonia filled the air as soon as you opened the door. My hairdresser was a Hispanic woman, but sported bright yellow blonde hair, carefully mani-cured as to not show any of her dark black roots. She sat me down on a black leather chair, put on a neon green bib and asked if I was going to have the usual haircut. The usual for me meant trimming about two inches from my hair and adding layers to add volume to my already thick, long hair.

That day I decided to rebel and have a change in my life. During that particular growth spurt, I had begun to question the standards of beauty that I had taken for granted my entire life. I was beginning to take on interest in the

THE REVENGE OF PINK PUFFY DRESS

When it was time to go to college, I applied to my hometown university. At the time, the university had a partnership with the local community college that allowed students to seamlessly transition from an associate's degree to a bachelor's degree. Neither of my parents had attended college in the United States, so I figured out what I had to do to obtain a partial scholarship and cover the rest of the tuition with student loans. Tuition at the time was about $500 per class, and, if I took five courses, the semester would cost me approximately $2,500. Thinking about that amount of money now as a working adult seems doable with the right budget and savings, but at the time it was not something that was readily available for myself, nor my parents.

I decided to major in Communications with the hopes of one day becoming a public relations specialist or broadcast journalist. I loved writing, reading and learning about people's lives, so it felt like a good fit. Before the first semester of my freshman year began, I started working for the student newspaper at the university as a reporter, and my first assignments ranged from freshman "Welcome Week" orientation to the Student Government Association (SGA) beat. I soon positioned myself as an involved student covering political issues on campus, and I had gotten to know a lot of the administration, including the school's president.

In April 2007, the university turned 15, and the institution's administration decided to celebrate this anniversary year with a *quinceañera*. They felt that the theme would be a celebratory and fitting representation of the area's culture and tradition. The university was planning to have a grand ball, and invite distinguished community members to feast and celebrate among school administrators and a select number of students. Fifteen students were chosen to represent the 15 *damas* as in a traditional *quinceañera*, and the SGA president was representing the main debutant. The 15 *quinceañeras* were escorted by 15 male students, representing the *chamberlanes*. I did not think much about it initially as my mindset on *quinceañeras* was the same as it had been when I was actually 15 years old.

However, one of the university staff members mentioned that each student would be paired up with a university sponsor, including representatives or owners of businesses in the area. The light bulb clicked immediately for me; this could be my opportunity to network and potentially land a summer internship. They even promised that this could possibly lead to scholarship donations for the next semester, so, I agreed to be in the presentation and rehearsed with the group at least twice a week before the big event. The university spent hundreds of dollars buying pink puffy dresses for all the female students and renting tuxedos for the young men. The day of party, we all had to wake up early and get our hair, nails and pedicure done, even though we were wearing white gloves that covered the majority of our hands and closed-toe shoes. The venue was dimly lit and the moment arrived when the hours of rehearsal were put to good use. In front of hundreds of school administrators, politicians and profitable donors, we waltzed away, swinging from side to side. After the dance, we all sat at a table in the back of the room and ate dinner.

I remembered the printed event program featured the logo of a local advertising agency, so I asked one of the university staff members to introduce me to the representative of the business. We approached a tall man with gray hair, pale blue eyes and a pink tan. His skin color looked like a lot of the other sponsors' in the room, but they all looked very different from the students who were entertaining them, including myself. He told me his name—I will call him Michael—and introduced himself as one of the presidents and founders of the advertising agency. Although he was accompanied by his wife and two of his colleagues, I was prompted to ask him to dance; I was wearing a ball gown, after all.

I was not entirely comfortable with asking an older man to dance because I wanted a professional relationship with him, and, honestly, that did not seem to me like the best way to start. I figured, however, that I needed to take advantage of the opportunity to get to know him, so I asked this very important man to an innocent dance. Wearing a tiara on my head, I reached out my right arm adorned with a white glove up to my elbow, while I smiled and introduced myself as one of the recipients of his company's scholarship, and I asked him if he would like to dance. Michael declined the dance, stating that his wife might be jealous, so I took the opportunity to ask him right there if he had any summer internships available for college students. He gave me his business card and told me to email him on Monday. I was elated at the thought of potentially soon being in a professional setting. I had not mentioned my work, and the only thing he knew about me was that I was a young Latina in a pink dress who asked him to dance; but that did not matter to me at the moment because I was ready to start training for my future career.

Three days later, on Monday, I did not wait a second after sunrise to start writing him an email. It was near noon by the time I actually sent it because I had put so much effort in trying to make it sound professional; "I am following up on our conversation from last Friday about applying for an internship at your advertising agency. As a Communications major and editor of the school newspaper, I am very interested in the position," I began the email. The next paragraph detailed my experience, and I ended it with "I would greatly appreciate an appointment for an interview; I am available from 8 a.m. to 8 p.m. Mondays, Wednesdays and Fridays, and can be reached by email. . . . Thank you for your time and consideration." Michael replied exactly 15 minutes later, asking me to meet him at the office for an interview that Wednesday.

SMOKE AND PLANTS

I arrived at an 1800s repurposed home with art deco inspiration for my internship interview. I was not sure whether to knock or to ring the doorbell, and if it had not been for the sign bearing the last names of the owners, I would have thought this was indeed someone's home. I decided to ring the doorbell, but no sound was apparent, so I knocked. I let myself into a dimly lit home with old wooden floors. The air was stale and it smelled like a bar at 1:30 a.m. with lingering layers of cigarette smoke on the walls. The reception area had black leather sofas, a modernistic red wall in the back and a collage of bricks on the other side. Also in the reception area, there was a Hispanic young woman—whom I will call Mary—with impeccable straight hair, wearing a spaghetti strap shirt and a tight pencil skirt. Mary called Michael on the phone and told him I was there to see him, then she asked me to wait, so I awkwardly sat on the chair next to her as I did not feel quite comfortable enough to sit on the sofas. It had taken me a while to decide on what to wear for the interview, especially since, as a college student, my closet consisted of mostly jeans and T-shirts. I did have a few stylish blazers, so I decided on a trendy, yet professional, red blazer and black slacks. I had also put some thought into my hair, and, Googling interview tips, I had decided on a clean slicked back bun because I did not want my hair to be a distraction.

Mary escorted me to Michael's office, which looked like it had at one point been the main bedroom or perhaps a living room of the old house. The room was adorned with another red leather sofa and some golf paraphernalia. Michael continued talking to his partner—I will call him Jason—and motioned for me to sit down. "Mary, will you get me a glass of water?" he asked the woman who had led me to his office. She walked off and came back with two glasses of water, then he asked if I was okay before telling her to leave. I do not remember what questions they asked me, but I do remember that they said they would not pay me. They offered to talk to one of my professors so I could receive college credit, but they were not going to compensate me financially. I was hoping to get paid so that I could make some money during the summer since the school newspaper did not have summer issues, and I did not want to have to find a summer job. I accepted the position anyway, convincing myself that I was going to have to figure out my finances later.

The agency had account managers and account executives, the people who oversaw the overall advertising business of several clients assigned to them. They were the ones who proposed a spending budget to the client on where and how they should be spending their advertising money, and, if the client approved it, then the creative part of the team would produce the content. This included writing radio and television scripts, designing print advertisements, as well as recording and editing television commercials. The agency also had people who placed and ordered these advertisements to different mediums, contacting the television stations, newspapers, magazines and radio stations, and coordinating when the advertisements would run and how much needed to be spent. When all was said and done, all the account managers did was tell the creatives and the purchasing department what to do. They were just the face of the agency, for the most part. There was even one staff member there just to facilitate the "traffic" in the agency processes, and she was the liaison between the creative team, the account managers and purchasing.

I learned everybody's roles mostly because I would walk around and ask people what they were doing and if they needed any help. As an intern, I really did not have much to do; everybody was busy doing their very specific task, that I was probably a bit of a disturbance. They did not want to take the time to teach me, but, during my first week, Michael assigned me to shadow one of the account managers, whom I will call Gilbert. Gilbert's account was a state bank, one of the agency's biggest clients, which has since closed down, and he was never around. I would often beg him to let me organize his assignment binders, and he would begrudgingly agree and ask that I not mess anything up. So after he gave me the first okay, I would often give myself trivial assignments, even organizing all of the files in his filing cabinet, chronologically filing everything for the previous five years. And when I ran out of files to organize, I found even more banal things to do like dusting and watering the a plant he had in his office. I have no idea how the plant even survived being in that smoke-filled room other than the attention that I gave it. Regardless, I enjoyed the agency environment, I appreciated that nobody really told me what to do, and I loved keeping myself busy and learning, so I continued to shadow everybody and ask them about their roles, even though they all had an inflated aura of self-importance that I felt only came with age and experience.

The agency seemed like an environment that fostered creativity and inno-vation. The office was always filled with salespeople who showered the staff with donuts and gifts. I noticed that the staff responded well to the gifts, and I wanted them to like me as well, so, even though I was not getting paid, I bought everybody donuts so that they would like me. Sometimes they would give me actual assignments translating advertisement copy from English to Spanish. I was in no way technically qualified to translate the documents other than I knew both languages from my bilingual upbringing. Spanish was my first language, and I spoke it with my family, and I learned English at school, but I never studied Spanish at school. The staff members at the agency assumed that because I knew it, I was qualified to translate copy into Spanish because, well, I was Mexican. The rest of the staff members had either never bothered to learn Spanish—even though more than 85% of the population in our border town spoke Spanish[1]—or they were White, and were simply not expected to know Spanish.

TOO MUCH MAKEUP AND SCANDALOUS HEADLINES

My interest for journalism had peaked in high school because I did not quite know how to talk to people, and, like most teenagers, I wanted to be liked. I always defined myself as quiet and shy, but working for the monthly high school publication meant that I had a mandatory excuse to talk to people, and the camera was my shield for any uncomfortable situation. With the excuse of taking photos and conducting interviews, I made a lot of friends in high school, and I looked up to the school newspaper editor—whom I will call Stacy—who was thin, had long blonde hair and was considered a top student. My junior year of high school, the editor-in-chief was graduating, and I had slowly taken up learning how to use the software to lay out pages and give her a break. On the last issue, Stacy asked me to design the entire paper as a test to see if I was fit to become the next editor. Although she was only a few years older than I was, her brisk walk, long blonde hair and punchy tone always intimidated me. I designed the pages of the last monthly publication that year, which took me hours to align every column, photo and illustration. On her last day, Stacy was coming back from taking her senior portrait, when she asked to look at the layout, and, even though she knew that I had done the work, she yelled, "Who the hell designed this? Who the hell *ruined* my paper?" I slowly approached her and nervously asked her what was wrong with it. She said everything was wrong and started deleting things. She deleted and reshuffled articles for about 15 minutes, then got up from the desk and said she did not have time to deal with stupid things and left.

That was my first experience feeling utterly inferior to someone else, and, after that, I decided that I was going to be a nicer, more diplomatic editor—because I did end up becoming the editor. I established lunch meetings for those who were not able to take the class, and I took a junior student under my wing to mentor her for the role once I graduated. I mentally decided I would thank the previous editor for teaching me everything I *should not* do. Except, I had not learned to be fearless. I wanted to be fearless like her, so, in my young way of thinking and attributing Stacy's braveness to her outward appearance, I dyed my hair blonde and grew it out as long as I have ever had it, trying to be like her, but I promised myself I would never treat others the way she made me feel.

Following this experience in high school, when it was time to decide on a college major, Communications seemed like the best fit. One of my friends had joined the weekly school newspaper at the university and recommended that I apply, so when the student advisor visited our classes to recruit student staff for the paper, I did not hesitate to join. So, during my freshman year of college, in addition to wearing pink dresses and tiaras at the university's *quinceañera*, I was diligently learning the ways of an investigative journalist. My first assignments were "Welcome Week" and the SGA, and I was more interested in covering the first. I still remember the lead from my first story: "You can smell the cooking hot dogs from a mile away, as staff prepares for Welcome Week." Our full-time staff advisor was a serious woman who had previous copy editing experience working for the Chicago Sun-Times, and she edited all of our articles before they were published. She took a look at the first sentence in my article and asked "Were they already cooking? Could you smell the hot dogs in the air from a mile away?" "No," I answered, "I was trying to embellish the story." "Then it's a lie," she said, and she unceremoniously clicked the delete button. That was the first time I truly learned about meaning of journalistic integrity, and while others took offense to her honest criticism, I looked up to her as a mentor, and strove for perfection as I learned from her.

The newspaper staff members had meetings every week to receive story assignments and also to talk about current events or even personnel issues. "You need to be beyond reproach," the advisor would council us, stressing that in order to uncover truths, we had to be able to live and work to a high standard. The university's student editor at the time was a young man who had been the editor of the high school paper before Stacy—I will refer to him as Mario. In high school, he was known for being a troublemaker, but Mario was now a "changed" man at the university. On my first day as a reporter, he was showing everybody photos of his trip to China, where he taught children how to speak English. He was on top of every hard-nosed investigative story of the university, so university staff members both feared and befriended him. Mario was also close friends with a student reporter—I will refer to him as Adam. The journalism community in our region was small at the time, and I had briefly met Adam in a journalism competition while in high school. Adam and Mario would sometimes make fun of the female reporters, referring to them as *sweetie* and telling jokes about how difficult it must be to be a woman. Adam once approached me before a staff meeting and said "You know, you would be much prettier if only you did not wear as much makeup as you wear now, and if you didn't dye your hair blonde. You look too fake." I was outraged and surprised that he actually voiced his thoughts out loud to me, but even more so that I allowed his words to make me feel self-conscious about my appearance because, a while later—perhaps with his comment in my sub conscience—I dyed my hair a darker shade and skipped the dark mascara.

As the youngest member of the group, I was always assigned stories that were considered boring by most other student reporters. I made the most of the stories, and tried to find an angle that would uncover some truth. I had a tactic all worked out; I would befriend the administrators' assistants, so that they would be more willing to schedule interviews for me. Then, when I requested to speak with them, I would mention that I wanted their interview to get *their* side of the story and that I was only trying to uncover *their* truth of the situation. Mario and Adam had a different approach; they questioned administration in an accusatory manner that would make them defensive and would often lead to controversy. They often got into wars with the SGA president, and they criticized his leadership in editorial columns. They relished each controversial moment, and boast whenever they were "cooking up" something "juicy."

The part of the job that most interested me was talking to people and finding a way to help them. I would make the best of the serious assignments, but what I craved for was personal stories that tug at the heart, so I came up with the idea of writing a series of stories about student struggles. The idea came from a feature I had written in high school about a student who had become paraplegic as a result of a car accident. Finding such heart-compelling stories was not easy, but it was a task that I had given myself to help me grow professionally.

Every Wednesday morning, the student editor reviewed our assignments. He would read each story pitch out loud, and the reporters were responsible for providing a status update. Toward the end of the semester, I was losing respect for both Mario and Adam, and I found myself rolling my eyes at their comments and at their attempts to sound professional every time the advisor came in the room. In one of these meetings, I was in particularly bad mood, so when the editor called out my regular assignments, and I just gave him my updates. Then he asked, "Are you ever going to find another piece for your student feature?" to which I nonchalantly responded with a "Yeah, yeah, yeah." The sides of his lips tensed, he instantly got up from his chair, and in the middle of the meeting he yelled, "You cannot talk to me like that! You cannot respond to my orders like that! I deserve respect!" I do not recall my answer, but knowing too well that he would never have behaved like this when addressing a male reporter, I remember that I left the room after that, feeling extremely upset.

The weeks to follow were not easy. Our advisor scheduled a meeting between the editor and me, and we came to the conclusion that we would try to get along while working on the newspaper. I explained that I had lost respect for him because of all of the inappropriate jokes that he and his male friend made before each meeting, and that, if he demanded respect, he would have to show respect for me as well. My "Yeah, yeah, yeah" had not been very professional, but it did not compare to the comments about my gender, hair or makeup. A few weeks later, Mario and Adam both announced their resignation and left the paper, so I was tasked to fill in as interim editor alongside another student staff member who had been there longer. By the end of the semester, I had turned in my application to become the next editor, and I was selected as the sole finalist.

Now, as the student paper editor, I decided to work alongside the new SGA students, a group that was often perceived as the paper's adversary, but

I found that negative relationship pointless. Instead, I assigned an SGA president's corner, and I would attempt to meet with them often to talk about the issues that the students cared about—they were student representatives, after all. During this time, there was a prominent gossip blog circulating our campus. The blog was not always credible and the stories were often written in crude language or symbolism. One day, I had lunch with one of the SGA male vice presidents to discuss such issues. For a brief second while we were sitting at the cafeteria, I felt self-conscious to be having lunch with a man, and I could feel some people curiously staring at us, but I shook the feeling away, and I continued talking to him about our work.

The next day, the newspaper advisor called me into her office, stating that there had been a story published in the gossip column about me and the SGA vice president. The story said that I liked to read the *Bible* with the vice president, and he liked to open up my pages, and the way it was written had nothing to do with an actual *Bible* or pages. I thought about writing an editorial column defending myself in my publication because I was really upset that someone would imply that the only reason why the SGA and the newspaper students were in amicable terms was because I was allegedly sleeping with the vice president. I decided to instead ignore it because it was not worth my time or energy, and, instead, I chose to always uphold myself to the highest standards. During my time as student editor, I got to meet President Obama, I asked Hillary Clinton about the border wall, and I gained the respect of the university administrators. Even though sometimes I felt like I was swimming against the current, I was actually building muscle for the tides to come.

LANDING THE JOB

The months after my internship, I had made a note to keep in touch with Michael at the advertising agency because I knew my graduation was on the horizon. I was set to graduate in December 2008, and I did not want him to forget about me. I also kept in touch with Gilbert and several of the graphic designers in the team even a year after my internship. Sometimes they needed talent to model in commercials, so they reached out to me to participate. As a college senior, I was always too busy, but I communicated with them anyway. In September 2008, I realized that I needed to start looking for jobs since I was going to be graduating in a few months, and I needed to start "planting my seeds," as all of my mentors and professors instructed me to do. By then, I had completed several internships, and, at 20 years old, I had a résumé full of experience that ranged from being a dental assistant to working at my beloved advertising agency.

I decided to send an email to Michael so that he may remember me. I did not want to sound desperate, so I Googled the company's website, and I noticed that they had redesigned it. This was a perfect excuse for an email, I thought. I titled the email subject "New Webpage Design," and simply said that I loved the new fresh look. Three minutes later, Michael replied, "Thanks. How are you doing?" then I responded 10 minutes later, and, after some thought, I casually said that I was great and graduating in December. I also mentioned owing a visit to the team with some donuts, a trick I had picked up from the salespeople, who were always invited to stay and chat with the agency staff long as they came bearing gifts for the team. He replied with "Congratulations. Still trying to make a living. Stay in touch."

I had not yet graduated college—I had one more month until I did—but with the news of harsh economic times, I was desperate to land any job that did not require me to work at a mall. A close classmate who had graduated a semester before me had spent the previous semester working at a retail store in the mall, and I did not want this to happen to me, so I was glad that the seed I had planted the month before had sprouted. I wanted desperately to work at a place that matched my degree, so after the "remember me" email that I sent Michael, I eventually talked to someone over the phone, and Michael scheduled for me to stop by his office to talk about my future in the company, giving me a part-time job by November. One of his staff members, Susy, was thinking of going back to college, so they needed a replacement for her, and, as I thought about what I wanted to do after college, I realized that at the student newspaper, the part I enjoyed the most was designing the layouts. Therefore, I had prepared a binder filled with sample designs from class and from my newspaper layouts carefully placed in covered sleeves.

Going back into the office, I was no longer greeted by Mary. Instead, Susy, an account manager, was sitting at the front desk. She called over to Michael, and I was escorted to his office. This time, it was Michael alone without his partner Jason. We made small talk, and I let my sample binder rest with me on my lap. I was just happy to be ahead of the game and work for an actual advertising agency. He then nonchalantly said that I could start as soon as possible and asked how much I was getting paid at the newspaper. I was making $10 an hour because I had applied to be in a special student program; the rest of the staff members were getting paid a bit above the $7.25 minimum wage. He said, "Alright, well, then, I'll pay you $13 an hour, is that okay with you?" I did not know what to say; I did the math in my head and $3 an hour more than what I was making sounded like a whole lot, so, without any argument, I meekly agreed to that salary. He smiled and thanked me as to end the interview process. I was a bit confused at the process, after all, he had not even seen my design samples. How would he know if I was any good at doing the job he was hiring me for? I asked Michael if he wanted to take a look at my design samples, and he chuckled and said that there was no need because he was not hiring me to be part of the design team. He, then, explained that a few people had had to leave the agency, including Mary, and that he needed someone to both do account management and to be able to pick up the phone and greet people. "Besides," he said, "you are far too nice to be a designer." I took a moment to think about what this meant, put my portfolio back in my purse, and agreed to take the job. How could I refuse an offer for a real job even if it was not quite in the track that I wanted? At the time, the only advertising experience I felt I had was the internship, and I did not think about negotiating my salary. The next week, I made arrangements at my student newspaper job and moved my schedule around to accommodate working part time until I graduated in December.

SHORT SKIRTS AND BIG BUDGETS

Since the agency was housed in an old repurposed home, the ceilings were low, the floors would creak and the windows hardly let in any light. On my first day, Susy was waiting for me in the front office. Then, she showed me the agency's organizational system for keeping track of jobs, the job jackets that are required for the designers, and the budget system for clients. She managed four clients, including a large car dealer that had about five dealerships throughout the Rio Grande Valley, in deep South Texas. Each month, the account manager was responsible for creating a budget, outlining all of the proposed advertising spending for the month, and getting the client to agree to the budget.

The media salespeople would flock the agency, instead of the client, so that the agency would recommend that specific medium channel or advertising avenue to the client. Each client had his or her spending limit, and how much the budget could be increased, and as Susy was explaining this process to me, another account manager walked in to drop off some paperwork to the front desk. Her stiletto heels echoed on the wooden floor as she walked toward us with her long exposed legs. She was wearing a short black skirt well above the knees—a good four to five inches below the hips—and a leopard print button-down shirt with the top four buttons unbuttoned showing a low-cut black undershirt. Francine, as I will call her, was somewhere between 50 and 60 years old, had a high-pitched nasal voice and always smiled as she talked.

When she left, Susy simply continued explaining the budget process and added that at the end of each month, the account manager was responsible for scheduling a budget meeting to propose the budget for the upcoming month. She added, "Romeo is the owner of the car dealership that we oversee. He will want to see and meet with Michael, but you should be a part of the meeting to hear what they are talking about and schedule out the advertisement. Make sure to have three copies of the budget available. Oh, and *wear a short skirt on budget days*. Romeo may increase the budget if you wear short skirts." I gazed at her face blankly because for a second I thought she might be joking, but she just smiled and continued explaining the reconciliation process after the invoices arrived. She was not joking, I realized. "Short skirts mean more money," the thought stuck with me for the rest of the day. I felt dirty even thinking about exposing my bare legs during a budget meeting to lure a client into spending more of their hard-earned money into an advertising budget that might or might not make any business sense. What were they going to get in return? I looked down at what I was wearing—black slacks and a button-down shirt. Part of me felt insulted, and another part of me swore to never wear a skirt or dress as long as I worked there.

I felt like I needed to get out of the building to get a breath of fresh air. Outside, I found Gilbert and another employee I had not met during my internship, both smoking cigarettes and talking. She introduced herself—I will call her Kathy—and gave me a welcoming look that encouraged me to get closer to her despite me fruitlessly trying to escape the smoke inside. I crossed my arms and looked down, asking how they were doing. I said I was so excited to start working at the agency with them, a natural thing to say when you start working somewhere new, I thought. Gilbert and Kathy eyed each other and Gilbert rolled his eyes; "How long do you think she is going to stay here?" asking Kathy as if I was not right there in front of them. "Oh, she is a lifer!" she looked at me from top to bottom and continued squinting her eyes while she huffed and puffed on her cigarette; "She's definitely a lifer." I asked what they meant, and they smiled as if they remembered that I had been there all along. Gilbert then said, "Oh, *sweetie*, you just look like you could spend the rest of your life here like Nora. She's been here forever." What I took that to mean was, "You don't look like you could go very far." They raised their chins and continued looking away as they finished their cigarette. In the days to come, both Kathy and Gilbert announced that they were leaving the company and had found better things to do. Gilbert had been offered a job with one of his clients, a local insurance agency that then dropped the advertising agency shortly after he began his job. Kathy got married and stopped working to the best of my knowledge.

MONEY TALK

Susy had also left the agency to finish her degree as a full-time student. I was singlehandedly working her former clients in addition to Gilbert's and Kathy's, and serving as a receptionist. The end of the month was arriving, so I scheduled a budget meeting with Romeo to overview the car dealer's budget. He walked into the office, and I introduced myself, welcoming him in, but he just half smiled and walked straight into Michael's office. I walked in behind him holding the stack of papers that I had prepared for the meeting, Michael greeted him, and they soon started talking about their golf tournaments. Michael offered him a cigarette, Romeo accepted it, and they both started smoking while talking about golf. I sat there next to Romeo, facing Michael, forcing a respectful smile on my face. I wanted to be successful in the advertising business, so I made a mental note to remember the gibberish they were blabbing about and to learn more golf terms. Michael pressed the intercom, called Francine—an account manager—and asked her to bring him and Romeo some coffee and water. A few minutes later, Francine appeared with the beverages and happily greeted Romeo, hanging around to chat with him a bit.

After a few minutes of the casual conversation, Michael explained to Romeo that I would be in charge of handling his account, but that he was still going to oversee it because Romeo was his best client and he deserved getting the "best treatment." Although I did most of the work, I was just another girl in the office, and was not "important enough" to have a meeting on my own with Romeo, is what I took from that. Romeo looked at me, smiled, and asked me how I liked working at the agency. I passed around the papers I alone had prepared, detailing the budget for the next month, then answered that I really enjoyed working there. Romeo said that he also really enjoyed spending time at the agency, and especially enjoyed talking to Michael. Then, he looked at me smiling and said, "I recently got a tattoo." I looked at him smiling, still holding the budget outline in my hands, patiently awaiting the discussion of the dollar amounts I would have to myself schedule because, by then, the purchasing department had also been let go. "Aren't you going to ask me where and what kind of tattoo I have?" Romeo continued. Michael chuckled and said, "Oh, there you go again, Romeo…" "Sure," I responded innocently, "what kind of tattoo do you have?" Without hesitation, he answered, "I have a tattoo of a $100 on my penis. Do you want to know why? Because I like to play with my money, I like to watch my money grow, and whenever my wife wants to spend money, I just tell her to blow money any time." Both him and Michael laughed, and Michael, chuckled something like, "You're going to scare this poor girl away, Romeo." "I'm just kidding," Romeo added, looking at me, "take it as an initiation into working here."

I stared at the papers I was holding and took a second to decide whether or not I was going to force a smile or fake laugh. I had seen this sort of behavior on television; the series Mad Men had just premiered on television, but it was set in the 1960s. Surely, this was not the way advertising professionals really behaved in the real world in the 2000s! At the time, I did not have cable, so I had only heard about the show, but had never watched it. Perhaps, I should have. I decided not to laugh nor smile after all, and continued passing around the rest of the paperwork. The remainder of the meeting, Michael explained the amounts of television advertisement being proposed, and tried to budget Romeo into spending more money on it. Romeo agreed, got up from his seat handing me back the copy of his budget, and left the room.

I never told anybody about this joke for years to come. Who could I tell? The president of the company himself was present in the meeting and thought it was just fine... I did not ask to switch accounts because it was understood that jokes like that are normal for male clients like Romeo to tell, and that one should just laugh at them and move along trying to get more business. I did, however, continue wearing pants to my meetings instead of dresses or short skirts. In the years to come, I cannot say that Romeo gained any more respect for me. I do not think that he respected anybody, for that matter. During those budget meetings, he would tell Michael outrageously embellished stories about golf or about the time that he accidentally urinated on his kitchen floor after a long night of drinking. He would often make fun of me for having a degree, saying that it was a waste of time. These experiences still make me cringe, especially when I am reminded of them driving around South Texas, and seeing the same billboard that I had secured for him 10 years ago.

A FRIENDLY FACE

After working at the agency for a few months, Michael realized that giving me more than seven full accounts in addition to making me a receptionist was not going to work. I was paying more attention to going to meetings and handling the accounts than answering phones and fetching coffee. He called Mary, the young woman who had been the receptionist when I was an intern a couple of years back, and offered her the job back. Mary had been working at a telemarketing call center, and gladly accepted the position back at the agency. She started only a few days later, and sat at the front desk. Because Gilbert and Kathy had left, there were two open rooms available for me; one in the front area, right next to the reception desk, the other in the back of the house. The first one had a huge window facing the front of the building and two large mesquite trees, while the other toward the back was windowless and next to Michael's office. I chose the front office. "Are you sure?" Michael asked, "Everybody can see you're there. You can't hide from anybody if they're looking for you." I would sacrifice hiding from people to being next to the cigarette chimney that was Michael's office. Even with two air filters, the entire building spread the smell of the daily pack of cigarettes he smoked.

Because my office was right in front of the reception area, Mary and I grew close. Mary really enjoyed working at the advertising agency; she did not complain when Michael would buzz her phone and ask her to bring him a cup of coffee or water. Even though the kitchen area and watercooler were five steps away from his office and the reception area was further away, Mary did it with a smile. I remember the time Michael asked me for coffee during my first weeks working at the agency, I blurted out, "Are you serious?" and he never asked me to fetch him coffee again, but he continued to requested it from Mary and Francine. I had learned to have self-respect, and did not find it appropriate for me to serve him water or coffee just because I was a young Latina in the office.

Mary was about three years older than I was, and she had not finished her degree, but also never mentioned going back to school in the years that I worked at the agency. She often wore spaghetti-strap shirts and sometimes short skirts. Though, more often than not, she wore tight jeans and flats. Her hair was long, dark and neatly flat ironed every day. The men at the office enjoyed speaking to her, as she would giggle whenever they made a joke. Often, I would talk to Mary when we had a slow day at the agency—there were many of those despite the several clients I had. I worked too quickly and then there was a lot of "hurry up and wait." She would step into my office, sit on the chair across from mine, and talk to me about the boy she liked, who would often not reciprocate her feelings. He would play power games, showing her affection one day, getting her to fall in love with him, and then ignoring her messages and calls for days.

Even though we were both Latinas around the same age, I did not know how to handle this type of situation well. The women with whom I would hang out in college were too preoccupied with their careers or would not give much thought to boys. If a guy did not reciprocate feelings, they would move on, and life was fine. But this was not the case for Mary, so I would give her what I thought was good advice, telling her to forget this guy, that she was worth all the love in the world, and that she did not need him to be happy. But I started noticing that whenever she would get back with him, she stopped talking to me. I later learned she did this because I had given her advice to stay away from him, and, since she was back with him, I was "not her friend." So, the next time that he broke up with her, I just listened, without giving her any advice. I changed the conversation or talked about trivial things she could relate to—like clothes—and that was the end of her cold shoulder.

Mary was someone Michael trusted and appreciated. I noticed that every day at 1 p.m., whenever Michael received a phone call, Mary would say that he was away in a meeting. Later, I noticed that Michael's vehicle was still in the parking lot, but his office lights were out. I approached Mary about this and asked her why Michael always had a meeting at that time, even though his car was still out there. "Oh, he likes to take naps after lunch. He tells me to take messages and to not disturb him during that time," she said, adding, "I actually have a funny story of the first time I started working here. Michael called me into his office and told me to take messages for any upcoming calls for the next hour. Then, he asked me to turn off the light. He went to the sofa in his office to lie down. Mind you, I was still in there! I had no idea what to do, so I froze; I was wondering if he wanted to *do something* with me as I turned off the light, but then Michael said 'What are you still doing here? I'm trying to nap!' I am so glad he was not trying to sleep with me."

THE NATURE OF THE BUSINESS

I managed seven accounts when working at the agency. As an account manager, I had to balance working the clients and working with the different sales people from different media outlets—television, newspapers, magazines, radio, and internet. During my time there, I realized that sometimes people say and do things without thinking about the context of their words. My male clients were very nice to me, but there was always some level of flirting. One of them casually placed his hand on my waist while showing me a product, and when I asked him what he was doing, it caught him off guard. He said that he did not mean anything bad by it, that he was just putting his hand on me, but I still was not okay with that. I had not given him permission to invade my personal space like this, after all, this was a business transaction.

Other sales people often came with gifts for people at the agency to persuade us into buying their media. Christmas time was a big deal and included all levels of gifting; the president of the agency would get multiple baskets full of wine, cheeses, and other delicacies. Gifts were a standard, but I still did not know how to interpret receiving so many chocolate gifts from a married salesman, until, he invited me to his condominium for the weekend. I asked if other people were going, including his wife, and he said no. I refused, of course, and stopped accepting gifts from him. Instead, I would simply thank him, and tell him that he could place the gifts in the kitchen area for the entire office staff to enjoy.

In addition to gifts, it was also very common to go out to lunch and take clients out to eat. With this, there was a line that needed to be balanced between professional work and social encounters, so I hardly ever invited my clients for lunch, unless I felt comfortable with him or her. Most of my meetings took place during office hours. I had a no-nonsense approach to the way I conducted business at the agency; if I felt that the client would not benefit from increasing the budget, I would often advise him or her against it. So, when I honestly saw an opportunity in advertising that they needed to

take advantage of, they knew I had an honest approach and that I was someone they could trust.

THE INTERNS

Each summer at the agency meant a new opportunity for college interns, just
I had once had only a few years back. Because I remembered that nobody
wanted to mentor these young students, I took it upon myself to oversee the
mentees and give them assignments. Michael was still in charge of selecting
the interns, so they sometimes landed in our office in mysterious ways. At
times, they were daughters of clients, other times, they were daughters of
prominent businesspeople in the area. But one thing was for sure, they were
always female, and they were *always* gorgeous. I noticed this trend when a
smart male newspaper coworker wanted an internship, was interviewed and
was not accepted. When asked why, Michael said "I just do not think he will
be a good fit for us."

Those beautiful young women who made the cut were, however, incredible people who are now successful professionals, and I am proud to have
been part of their journey. Because I had so many accounts, I always had
plenty of work for them to do, and I made sure to involve them in the
process. I completely trusted their abilities and they never disappointed.
When I was intern, I remember I did not even have a desk nor a computer of
my own, so, when my interns arrived, even though they shared the little room
I called office with me, I did not mind it because I watched them grow right
before my eyes. After they left, I happily wrote letters of recommendation for
them, and I still keep in touch with them.

THE WOMEN WHO BELIEVED IN ME

The beauty of having so many accounts to manage was that they were all
diverse, ranging from plastic surgeons, to car dealers, to a charter school, to a
fried-chicken restaurant. Not all of my clients were male, but all of the men
looked at me the same way. During my first meeting with a plastic surgeon,
his first comment to me while talking about the budget was "You know that
the problem on your nose can be easily fixed. We don't even need to do
surgery; I can just place a little bit of a filler right here," he said as he pointed
to the groove in between my eyebrows. Another time, after I had joined the
gym, he noticed saying "Ah, it looks like you have joined a gym! I can see
your waist now!" I had grown so accustomed to comments like these—
always focusing on what I should wear and what I should look like—that I
did not even process them anymore. It was as if these remarks never existed.

In fact, it takes me a while to remember them because it is easy to think that this was just the way things go.

The female clients, however, were another story. One day, the area manager of the fried-chicken restaurant was going to be in town for a public relations promotional campaign. I had a fearful level of respect for her. One of my first interactions with her was when she asked me to write a press release. Coming from a journalism background, this was an easy task. After emailing it to her, she called my office, "There is a typo in your press release! I don't have time for typos! I pay the agency to do its job." Instead of correcting her or defending the agency, I opened the document, asked if she was talking about the missing comma, and she responded "Yes, I don't have time to be checking for missing commas!" "Okay," I replied calmly, "it will not happen again. The document is fixed on my end and it is on its way to you. Can I help you with anything else?" And it did not happen anymore.

The day she was in town, I noticed that she did not ask for things, she demanded them, and all the men either feared her or disliked her. I, on the other hand, admired her. I told myself to take a mental note of her confidence and try to mimic it because I had somewhat forgotten how to assert myself, hiding behind customer service meekness. In my time working on her account and in my experience speaking to her, I always felt like she thought that I was weak, so I believed that she did not like me, and that I was a young bothersome person who did not know what she was doing. Until one day, she called my office and offered me a job. I politely declined it because, even though I was flattered by the offer, I did not believe in the core mission of a fried-chicken restaurant, so I offered to recommend someone else I trusted.

Another client, the charter school, also had very strong-willed powerful women who did not take any nonsense. They expected results, began a meeting with conversations only about the product and never about golf or drunken nights. They also offered me a job in their marketing department, which I declined, and that very year the charter school dropped the advertising agency, instead hiring a marketing professional to do the work in-house. I turned the job down because I soon left the advertising agency and found a position with my alma matter as a senior editor for the marketing department.

In this new position, I was finally making a respectable amount of money for someone with my experience, and I had an incredible supervisor, Camilla, who encouraged me to take on learning opportunities and leadership positions. She was the one who pushed me to start my master's degree because I had been mulling over the idea for years. She was also the one who encouraged me to study abroad in Brazil, which meant I could finally go on my very first airplane ride—something that in more than 25 years of my life I had yet to do—visiting an unknown city, figuring things out by myself in a language I did not speak. Thorough most of my career, she has been there encouraging me. So, a few years later, always taking advantage of opportunities to learn and grow, I eventually accepted a position as the university's Executive Director of Alumni Relations, while still in my 20s.

SHORT HAIR IN A MALE-DOMINATED FIELD

On January 1, 2017, I moved to Austin, Texas a few months after getting married. One of the first things I did following the move was cut my hair the shortest it has ever been—even shorter than when I turned 14. At age 30, I felt like I needed to let go of the weight of the stereotypes that the long hair represented. My long, naturally dark-brown hair was down to the end of my ribcage. I looked for the closest hair dresser and I booked the appointment. Until then, when I lived in South Texas, I had been going to the same hairdresser for more than 15 years, and, whenever I would mention going short, she would reluctantly cut it just a few inches shorter, never a bold cut.

I arrived at the bright pink repurposed home with a cat sitting in the front of the salon. The hairdresser had bright blue hair, a red bandanna tied around her neck and an array of colorful tattoos that covered most of her body. I was definitely not in South Texas anymore, and, when I asked her to cut it short, she did. I had it cut up to my ears, and I loved it! I felt that my hair was a reflection of how mature and professional I had become. After moving to Austin, I found a job (my current job) in a municipal department that can be typically male-dominated. Over 90% of my coworkers are men, several of whom are former police officers or men who used to work in the construction field.

I have been in my position for over a year, and I have since let my hair grow, not because I want long luscious hair, but because having short hair requires a lot more upkeep. I have surrendered to quickly placing my hair in a bun and stopped worrying so much about what my looks, my gender or my heritage mean to others. Instead, I have taken an introspective look at what it all means *to me*. Throughout all the twists and turns that I have had in my career and my personal experiences, I have found the value in taking owner-ship of how *I choose* to define myself and what that definition, in turn, means both for my career and for how I can help others. It took me a long time to come to the conclusion that advertising, public relations and fundraising all meant I wanted to help others, and I can now do it by working as a public servant in the municipal government.

Thanks to being Latina and growing up in a border town, I understand the value and importance of speaking more than one language. I also understand the hindrance of having limited English proficiency, and it is something that I am conscious of and actively deal with in my workplace. As a woman work-ing in a male-dominated field, I have learned to trust my education and my professional experience, and to surround myself with individuals and a work setting that are accepting to all people. I relish working in an area with positive rules, a true human resource department, and with empowered male and female leaders who trust my work and leadership. I sought after this feeling for a long time, and I am grateful to have found it.

I have also learned that the work environment that I experienced a decade ago is not the norm, and it should not be what is *expected*. I remember thinking that I deeply disliked working there, and I resigned saying that I wanted to further my career. I do not feel victimized nor resentful for the comments or jokes that I heard, but I am glad that I can internally identify that I do not want to work in an environment like that because it is not okay—an environment that encourages women to expose their legs to increase profits, that allows jokes about genitalia to the new staff members in the name of job initiation, and an environment that makes you feel uncomfortable for being born a woman instead of a man.

NOTE

1. U.S. Census Bureau (2016). *QuickFacts: Brownsville City, Texas*. Retrieved from https://www.census.gov/quickfacts/fact/table/brownsvillecitytexas/INC110216.

Chapter Five

Overcoming Biases
and Moving Forward

Cynthia S. Halliday

My maternal grandparents immigrated from Portugal to Brazil during the European Great Depression in the mid-1930s. My grandmother was pregnant at the time my grandfather moved to Brazil, so she stayed in Portugal until their first daughter was born. A few months after she gave birth, she and her baby daughter joined my grandfather in Brazil. On the other side, my paternal grandparents were born and raised in very humble conditions in Brazil and were married when still in their teenage years. My paternal and maternal grandparents were all dedicated parents who wanted to safeguard a better life for their children than the ones they had experienced. Both of my grandmothers worked as seamstresses in the earlier years of their marriages while raising their children, and one of them became a highly sought after seamstress in the city of Rio de Janeiro.

Both of my parents also worked full time and as a young child, as far as I can remember, my parents found joy in their careers. My mother worked as a sales account manager for a local branch of a multinational organization, and I have memories of her talking about how interesting her meetings were and how motivating it was to achieve her monthly goals. She also had exciting and fun stories about her colleagues, her supervisors, and her employees. My father did not seem to have any issues with her working either, so there was support from him. When they were recently married, my father had a stable position in the banking industry, but, as an entrepreneur at heart, he decided to open his own construction company, a profession he relished until he retired. During my childhood, my parents were financially well-off, which allowed me to attend private school.

√itnessing my parents work and learning about the legacy my grandparents had left to their families, I never questioned my ability of having a successful career while caring for my family. Never had I considered issues related to any type of discrimination at work. At the age of 13, following the suggestion of my sister, who was 23 at the time, I made the decision to apply for a technical high school. I had to prepare myself to take a very intensive and competitive exam to be accepted into the program, but after preparing for several months, I took the day-long exam and I was thrilled when I found that I had made the list of those few who had been accepted into the school. Although I had always been a good student during my elementary and middle school years, this was my first experience in a competitive selection process. At that time, only my exam scores were to be considered for acceptance into the school. There was no gender, racial, or income quota; there was no evaluation of my past educational performance and no letters of recommendation written on my behalf. The competitive exam was the only measure used to test my proficiency and preparation to study at the school. I was excited with the prospective of studying science, more specifically, food technology, and I had the full support from my family.

During the four years of technical high school, I enjoyed every aspect of the fields of science and technology. I was also very active in sports at the time, and I was able to balance school with competitive sports. I have great memories of those wonderful years and I cannot recall any incident that sparked feelings of being discriminated against due to my gender. It was not until after I graduated from the food technology program, at the age of 17, and was making plans to attend college, that I recall being faced with any type of gender stereotypes or biases.

TRUST THOSE WHO TRUST YOU

The first memory I have of encountering stereotypes related to my career direction was when I was in my late teenage years. After four years of technical school, learning the science of food, I was determined to advance my education in the field by pursuing a college degree in Food Engineering. One of the few universities that offered this degree was located out of state and it was one of the top five universities in the country. Meanwhile, I also had the opportunity to apply for a Biomedicine program at a local university—where I was accepted—and, due to the excitement of being officially a college student, lost focus of the direction that I had originally intended to follow. I decided to start my studies of Biomedicine and forgot, temporarily, about the idea of applying to the out-of-state university that offered the degree that I had originally planned to pursue.

After a little over a year studying Biomedicine, I realized I had made a mistake. I remember the day I was chatting with my cousin, who was also a student in the Biomedicine program, and explaining to her that I was not happy with the direction that I had taken. I could see her love for the medical field, and I was able to recognize that because it was exactly how I felt when I was studying food technology. However, I never felt that way when studying Biomedicine. I knew it was not what I wanted to do with my life, so I left school that day determined to go back to my original plans. I had an honest conversation with my parents about my decision, and they supported me in my choice to apply to the Food Engineering program in the state of Sao Paulo. My family and I knew that it would not be easy to be accepted into the program, but my parents supported me in the decision to give it a try, which meant stopping college and spending six months preparing for the two-wave week-long exams.

So, I dropped out of my Biomedicine studies and dedicated one full semester to studying and getting ready to apply to the Food Engineering degree in one of the most reputable universities in Brazil: Universidade Estadual de Campinas, also known as UNICAMP. At the time, the process of admission was very similar to the one I had experienced when applying to the technical high school. Once again, there were no quotas for minority students, there was no evaluation of past educational performance, there was no letter of recommendation requirement. The only thing that counted was my overall grade in the extensive and competitive examination called Vestibular. And so, I started my preparatory studies for the UNICAMP Vestibular. In addition, one could only apply to a particular program (e.g., Mechanical Engineering, Medical School, Language Studies, etc.) at a single university at a time. If a candidate was not accepted into the chosen program at the chosen university, he or she would not be accepted into college at all that year. Considering that the Food Engineering program at UNICAMP was ranked number one in the nation, I knew it would be extremely competitive, but I pressed on and did not let it discourage me.

One day, after having spent months studying all disciplines I had learned in high school, I was sitting at home in the living room when I overheard a conversation between my father and a close relative, in which my father was telling him about my plans to apply to UNICAMP. Then, I never forgot what my relative told my father, "You should prepare Cynthia for the low likelihood of her being accepted into UNICAMP. She is competing against many Asian boys who live in Sao Paulo and her chances of being accepted are very small." Brazil had at the time the largest group of Japanese people living outside of Japan, more specifically in the state of Sao Paulo. There was a widespread stereotypical belief—not necessarily accurate—that the Japanese immigrants and their descendants performed much better in competitive examinations than the rest of the Brazilian population. However, although when preparing myself for the competitive exam I never considered that to be a threat, believing that I could also prepare myself to perform well, I was taken aback by the comment that I had overheard. I was upset, and I do not remember what my father said afterward, but he never told me about it and he never implied that I had low chances of being accepted at the university. Despite this incident, my parents continue to support me, and I felt even more motivated to succeed. I think this was the first time that my intellect was challenged based on my gender and ethnicity.

I did it; I got in! I found my five years at UNICAMP very fulfilling. I enjoyed immersing myself in the sciences of chemistry, biochemistry, physics, food technology, plant designs, production processes and so forth. I was officially the first female engineer in my family, and I was assured that neither gender nor ethnicity relate to one's capacity to learn and succeed in the science, technology, engineering or mathematics (STEM) fields. In my studies, I engaged with both male and female students, and I never felt any gender discrimination while in college. One of the things I learned is that anyone has very good chances of succeeding if they put their heart into their goals. I understand that some people may have more opportunities than others based on their early life challenges and experiences, but one's intellect is not defined by his or her gender, country of origin, or language spoken. I also learned that there will always be people who will believe in your capacity to succeed. My parents believed I was capable, and that was enough for me to pursue my dreams.

STEREOTYPES AND BIASES ARE NOT ALWAYS INTENTIONAL

Although I was not exposed much to gender discrimination and biases in the early years of my life, I did experience them in my career, particularly after I moved out of my native country. After graduating from college and working for a little over a year at a multinational firm in Brazil, I realized that I needed to improve my English language skills to progress in my career. I was young enough to take the risk of leaving a promising job in Brazil and move to the United States to develop my English skills and continue my education. Soon after I arrived in the U.S., I was introduced to the idea of pursuing a master's degree in Business Administration (MBA). I knew that I had a long way to go before I could be accepted into a reputable school that would provide me with the skills I needed in my career. First, I had to pass the language test required from non-native speakers. Second, I had also to pass the Graduate Management Admission Test (GMAT), which is an exam that tests the candidate's analytical, writing, quantitative, verbal, and reading skills and is required from anyone applying to a high-quality MBA program in the U.S, regardless of if he or she is a native-English speakers. Third, I had to complete my application profile, which included letters of recommendation and work experience, among other items, and it needed to be strong enough to be competitive.

After one year of dedication, studying and preparing myself for these exams, I received the exciting news that I had been accepted into the full-time MBA program at a highly ranked university in the U.S. Having always been a dedicated and well-performing student in my native country, I confess that I was not too concerned about my ability to succeed in graduate school. Having been in the U.S. for over a year, I also felt comfortable enough speaking English, although anyone who studies a foreign language eventually finds out that learning a new language is a lifetime commitment. But little did I know how much I still had to learn, and it was not until I started the MBA program that the reality of pursuing a graduate degree in a second language hit me.

My first semester in graduate school was particularly challenging. I was not only still developing my English skills, but also learning an array of business terms and jargons that I had never been exposed to, not even in my native language. My background in technology and engineering did not help much. During my first semester in the master's program, I spent several hours reading case studies with a dictionary by my side. Most of the time I had to read the same case more than twice to be able to understand it well enough to contribute in class discussions. During group discussions, I often felt overwhelmed and sometimes I could not follow the arguments and debates among my group members. I was feeling discouraged.

During the first semester, I also felt the pain and challenges that minority members feel. First, it was clear that the number of female students and of international students—two categories that I represented—were considerably small compared to American and male students. I was undoubtedly a minority for the first time in my life. Second, the school also encouraged in-group diversity, which meant that each group, usually composed of four or five members, had to have at least one female and one international student. In my group, I was both; I was the only female and the only international student.

When I look back at that experience, I think this procedure, which is followed in many other graduate schools in the U.S., is a disservice to minorities and to the other students in the cohort. Minority members already have to overcome many barriers, such as language skills, cultural differences, stereotypes and biases, so I believe that isolating them from those who may be more like them creates further issues. However, there were also many opportunities to learn from the local students. Some group members, particularly the ones who had lived abroad and had experienced the same feelings of frustration, tended to be more patient toward minorities. Others, not so much. There were those who just pretended I was not there, and there were some who noticeably wondered how in the world I had been accepted into the program. Sadly, I believed that in their mind, my lack of ability to communicate effectively was somehow a reflection of my intelligence. The language barrier was also affecting my self-confidence. I confess that I had thoughts of giving up; however, quitting was not an option for me as I had gone long ways to get where I was. I was determined to do all I could to learn and develop myself, and to succeed.

The same feelings of insecurity and lack of belonging were felt while I was in class, where I also struggled. MBA students are expected to contribute to the class discussions by sharing personal experiences or thoughts related to the topics being discussed. When I was in school in Brazil, I had always been outspoken; I enjoyed participating in class debates and sharing my opinions. However, my line of thought was not as easily communicated in English when I was in graduate school, so I avoided participating in class. When I had to contribute to the discussions, I had to really think through each sentence before opening my mouth. In my first semester, I did not feel comfortable participating in class, but I did the best I could at the time.

Eventually, things started to get better, and, in my second semester, I felt more comfortable with the topics and with my business language ability, which allowed me to act more like myself in school. During the summer, I further developed my language and business skills while doing my internship at a local branch of a multinational organization. I was even asked to continue working as a part-time intern at the organization during my second year of graduate school, which I did. I am glad I did not give up in my first school year, and I am thankful for those who supported me during the difficult times. I also realized that, although hindering, my English language ability was not a true reflection of my intellectual aptitude.

Unfortunately, there will always be people who will evaluate your intelligence based on your outward language ability. Several of my foreign colleagues in graduate school, particularly the ones who came from non-English speaking countries, felt the same way I did, complaining that some students ignored their comments. This type of stereotype, that is, when colleagues look at immigrants as not being qualified or not being "smart enough" because of their language skill is not uncommon, but I have only been exposed to it because I made the choice to get my graduate degree in a foreign country. I had never thought about it when I was going to college in my native land. When I was in college in Brazil, I had a few friends who were international students from Spanish-speaking countries, but I do not remember looking at them as less intelligent based on their language skills. In fact, I considered them very smart for their ability to earn a college degree in a non-native language, and I also enjoyed learning about their diverse cultures.

Despite some of the stereotypes and biases that I experienced in graduate school, there were many students who actually appreciated our differences, and were accepting and willing to help international students throughout the program. It is important to understand that either in life, in school or in our careers, we will always find those who are accepting of differences and those who will support us, and want us to succeed. While in graduate school, I developed lifelong friendships with American citizens who were willing to assist me in the beginning of the program, and who were appreciative of the cultural richness that I and my non-native classmates brought to class. I had friends who would frequently invite me over to study topics that I struggled with. I had professors who used their precious time outside of class to teach me things that I could not understand. I appreciate the administrative personnel of the school, who believed that we—international students—could and would succeed despite the difficulties we faced. By the time I earned my MBA, I had made lifelong friends in this new country. We learned from each other and we appreciated each other's differences. I am grateful for the memories that I have of those years in graduate school and from the difficulties I faced, which contributed to my personal and professional development.

As if these experiences in school were not enough, stereotypes and biases have also been present in my daily life experiences. On one occasion, my husband and I were looking for a house to rent. We were in transition, so we needed a place to rent for a year, and I was actively looking for a house close to work to avoid a long commute. One day, I saw an advertisement for a house that was just what we had been looking for. It was near my work location, and it was listed for a one-year lease. The advertisement had just been posted online and my husband and I agreed that it would be worth looking at the house. I called the real estate agent listed on the ad, and, when he answered my call, I told him that I was interested in the house and that I would like to schedule a visit. He reluctantly said that he had taken several applications at that point and that he was not taking any new ones.

I do not know why, but I was suspicious of his response. In my mind I wondered, "Did he say that because I have an accent? Did he say that because I am a woman?" I called my husband, who was born and raised in the U.S., and explained to him what had happened and how I felt about it. I asked my husband if he could call the real estate agent and ask to see the house, just to check if he would get the same information that I had gotten. He called him right away and was able to schedule a viewing on that same evening. The real estate agent also asked my husband to bring an application form. My husband and I were stunned! We visited the house, however, we decided not to rent it. I wish that I had had the guts to ask the agent why he did not take my application when it was evident that he was still accepting them, but, maybe because I had in a way become numb to such reactions from others, I kept quiet, and I will never know why I was not eligible, in his mind, to rent the house.

On another similarly disconcerting occasion, I was having a conversation with my neighbor when he asked me about my occupation and work responsibilities. At the time, I had a dream job; I traveled the world frequently and met wonderful people from all backgrounds and nationalities. I worked for an organization that provided an attractive work environment and benefits. When my neighbor learned more about my work responsibilities, he looked at me somewhat surprised and asked, "What makes you qualified for this position? Being a foreign professional should not be enough to qualify you for the job you have!" Taken aback by the question, I did not know what to say once again, nor do I remember what I said. After that informal conversation with my neighbor, a White male much older than I was, I asked myself if he would have questioned my (White American) husband the same way if he had been the subject of the conversation. Would my neighbor have challenged my husband's qualifications for his job? I will never really know, but, somehow, based on the compilation of gender-, ethnicity- and age-related biased incidents that I have experienced, I doubt it.

Certainly, I was not the only one facing these intolerant attitudes, and such negative behaviors are not exclusive toward foreigners. In my professional experience, I have also witnessed biases and stereotypes against some older female colleagues. For example, I had a female employee who was extremely hard working and intelligent. She had years of management experience and she was now in a stage of her life where she just wanted a part-time job to keep herself busy while earning some income. She had a passion for what she did, and she was fully dedicated to the success of our institution's programs. She was also older than the average employee in the organization. Once, I heard a (not-so-young) male employee comment on my female colleague's capacity to work productively because of her age, and I was appalled by his comment. Would he think the same about a male leader of the same age as my female employee? Would he have challenged a male leader's ability to perform in his leadership role due to his advanced age? The often-inflated sense of male superiority I have observed in the workplace, would lead me to not think so. My female employee was exceptionally productive and her knowledge and willingness to serve were a great asset to the organization. This female professional was probably one of the most effective employees we had in our office.

Cultural biases are also prevalent. On another occasion, when I was living in Spain and visiting a partner university, one of our young American students who was part of the group—and who happened to speak Spanish fluently—approached a female school director, put his arm around her shoulders, and started talking to her in Spanish. This was the first time the student met the female director. My husband immediately looked at me and said, "He would never have done that in the U.S. with a female professor." Afterwards, my husband and I discussed some potential reasons for the difference in attitudes. Was it a cultural bias? Was it a combination of cultural and gender biases? Would his behavior have been an unconscious (or conscious) feeling of gender and/or cultural superiority? Although it was obvious that the female director did not feel threatened by the American student's attitude, this student would likely not have behaved the same way in his own cultural setting.

There has been plenty of evidence of biases against gender, age, ethnicity, and race in all aspects of life. Yet, I believe that, in certain situations, biases rise unintentionally or from lack of cultural or situational awareness. One of my past work responsibilities involved serving on boards of directors, and, as the representative of a sponsoring organization, I had been invited to join the board of a non-profit international organization. We had monthly conference calls to discuss issues and topics related to the organization's goals and to plan annual activities. Once a year, we also gathered together in person to meet new board members and discuss future goals for the organization. There were about 20 members on this board of directors. In my first face-to-face meeting with my fellow board members, I noticed that I was visibly one of the youngest members of the board, if not the youngest. I was also the only female and the only international member of the board. One of the topics discussed in this initial meeting I attended was the replacement of board members who were retiring or otherwise leaving the board for other personal reasons. Several new names were brought to the table by the board members. I found it interesting that all the names recommended were those of male Americans, yet the organization was focused on increasing its membership outside of the U.S. At one point, I proposed that if we wanted to attract more international members to the organization, we needed to consider inviting more international members to the board. I added that in many locations, both in the U.S. and internationally, the presence of women leaders in national and international organizations is also increasing substantially and that we should consider inviting more female leaders to the board of directors.

Being a new member on the board, I did not know what reaction to expect from my fellow board members, some of the nicest people with whom I had interacted in my career. They looked at each other, as if they were surprised to not find any other female or international member on the board. Immediately, several members started suggesting names of potential board members who were located internationally, and some of them ventured some female names as well. Over the years, I have enjoyed my interactions with these board members, from whom I learned considerably, and I witnessed the increase in diversity on the board. I realized from this experience that some of the perceived unfair biases are unintentional. I also recognized that, as members of minority groups, we are in a better position and can take advantage of these types of situations to educate others, in non-confrontational ways, of unfair, albeit unconscious, biases.

Indeed, I was guilty of these involuntary biases at one point in my life when living in Brazil, and I can relate to that lack of awareness. I had a privileged upbringing in my native country; I was raised in a prosperous area of the city, and, until the end of middle school, I studied in reputable private schools. In Brazil, I was not considered part of a minority group and it was not until after I moved to the U.S that I realized that several people looked at me as "Brown-skinned," Latina, or Hispanic (even though I am not part of the latter group). It was only after I moved to the U.S. that I realized that my perceptions of race and ethnicity were not the same of others'. I suddenly became a minority in many ways. I was an immigrant; I was considered to have Brown skin, I was Latina, and gender became more salient to my identity, particularly when related to my career aspirations. Recently, while having dinner with my husband and my two young children, my 10-year-old son asked me if my skin was Brown. He looks just like me and I wondered why he asked me this question since it was not a notion that I had ever considered at his age. Growing up in Brazil, the color of my skin was a non-issue as I have always been considered White and part of the majority group, and maybe that is why I had never deliberately tried to connect with a particular group of people based on any sort of minority classification. Thoughts such as "Hey, let's hang out with so and so because he or she is Black, or Brown, or unprivileged," never crossed my mind, and it was natural for me to have friends from diverse backgrounds, races, and ethnicities.

DEVELOPING MYSELF AND CULTIVATING RELATIONSHIPS

Certainly, we will meet people who will challenge our abilities, who will question our achievements, who will doubt our contributions. However, I have met and worked with more people who have supported and respected me than otherwise. In my previous jobs, when I was faced with adversities, either related to the job itself or to work relationships, I found support and strength from those with whom I interacted daily. I have had the honor of working with several talented, caring, and positive colleagues in my career, both male and female, who were not blinded by stereotypes related to gender, race, ethnicity or nationality. I am also fortunate for working with leaders who have appreciated my contributions and who found value in what I did.

On one occasion, when I was attending a conference at my organization, I saw a colleague who worked in a different department. Although we did not work in the same area, we had worked together on several projects. He approached me and asked if I was interested in participating in an international assignment that would take me abroad for a period of about three months. He explained that the person who had been originally assigned to this appointment had had an emergency and would not be able to leave the country. He added that I had about eight months to get ready, and that I could take my family with me. He had intended to call me to discuss the opportunity but since he saw me at the conference that day, he decided to invite me then.

After discussing the opportunity with my husband, we accepted the invitation to take the international role, though I still needed to get a final approval from my supervisors. I was thrilled when I was given the permission to live in Spain for three months with my family to work on this assignment, while also working remotely to fulfill my work responsibilities from my regular job in the U.S. What they did not know at the time, however, was that I was almost three months pregnant with my second child. My spouse and I took that into consideration and we still decided to move forward with this new adventure, believing that the chance of having childbirth complications were minimal. Furthermore, I never considered pregnancy to be an impediment to fulfill my job responsibilities, although I acknowledge that women are different and I empathize with the ones who have complicated pregnancies. My husband was also committed to helping with our newborn daughter and three-year-old son while living in Spain and to also working on some assignments for the organization. When we were preparing ourselves to move to Spain, some people asked me how I dared taking a newborn baby to live in another country. My answer was simple, "Babies are born every day, everywhere in the world, and, in Spain, we will have the same medical facilities and other first-class resources to provide for the needs of our family." In a way, I felt connected with my maternal grandmother, who several decades earlier, had traveled alone with her two-month-old daughter by boat to an unknown country to start a new life. Her courage inspired and strengthened me in my new, albeit short, adventure. Fortunately, everything went well, and two months after my daughter was born we were landing in Europe.

My experience in Spain was more than fulfilling, though it was not without troubles. Each member of our family experienced the challenges of moving and living abroad, especially as I was working two jobs while caring for a young family. In my first month in Spain, I was sleeping an average of four to five hours per night. My husband did not speak any Spanish and had to adapt to the new life in Spain while caring for our children and working part-time. My son was patiently trying to get used to his new school environment and learn a language that he was not familiar with, and my two-month-old daughter was just a happy baby. Despite the challenges we faced individually and as a family, I never regretted the decision to have accepted this appointment. If I were offered the same opportunity today, I would not think twice and would accept the challenge all over again. We met several amazing people in Spain, visited fantastic places throughout the country, and immersed ourselves in an unfamiliar culture that will always be part of our lives.

A month after arriving in Spain, I received an email from my direct supervisor, stating that he would like to schedule a videoconference meeting with me. Initially, he had intended to meet with me in person, but since I was across the Atlantic Ocean, a virtual meeting would suffice. I was curious and nervous, and constantly wondered what it could be about. My supervisor assured me that it was a positive meeting, nothing that I needed to be concerned about. I was speechless when, in the meeting, I was presented with an organizational-level award from my supervisor and his direct supervisor for the work that I had done for the organization. I was overcome with joy and gratitude; I was not expecting anything like this.

Reflecting on these experiences, I realize that there are people everywhere in the world who are kind and will appreciate one's hard work and dedication despite of their differences. There are accepting and supportive leaders who will overcome any stereotypes and will appreciate the diversity that their employees bring to work. Whenever I am faced with biases or stereotypes in my personal or professional life, I try to remember the positive experiences I have had in my career and the amazing opportunities that I have been given. Those are reminders that we can overcome the challenges associated with gender, cultural, and other types of stereotypes.

I have also had supervisors who have gone out of their way to help me grow and develop in my career. They ensured that I attended top executive meetings, and they gave me opportunities to be in the spotlight, always in a positive way. When a project I suggested was successfully implemented, these true leaders ensured people were aware of my accomplishments. They also trusted and supported my ideas even when it was not always clear how things would work out. They provided me with opportunities to develop myself professionally and to continuously grow in my career. They went out of their way to protect me against biases and stereotypes from others when necessary. In some ways, I believe their support was their way of demonstrating appreciation for my work and for my dedication to the organization. The reaction was mutual; I also supported them in their efforts, I respected their positions and guidance, and I sought to help them succeed in their responsibilities. I will forever be grateful for the exemplary leaders I had in my career.

INSPIRING AND HELPING OTHERS ON THE WAY

In my role as a supervisor, I have tried to emulate the same support that I have received in my career when dealing with my employees. I have had the opportunity to supervise outstanding people and I wanted them to have the same opportunities that I have had in my career. I encouraged them to implement their ideas, I invited them to attend executive meetings where they had opportunities to discuss their job responsibilities, I gave them credit for the remarkable work they performed. I also wanted them to develop their own leadership skills, and I provided them with autonomy to make important decisions. The respect was mutual as well; they were satisfied with their jobs and they contributed immensely to the organization. We all enjoyed an environment of respect and cooperation, we shared our ideas openly, we did not fear criticism from our colleagues, and when we disagreed, we did so respectfully. I maintain contact with most of these former employees even years after we have no longer worked together. I can truly say that I have developed long-lasting relationships with many of my colleagues, supervisors, and subordinates.

After spending several years in corporate and other management positions, I made the decision to leave my full-time job, go back to graduate school to earn my doctorate degree in Management, and pursue a career in higher education. One of my responsibilities in academics is to teach graduate and undergraduate students, so, in my teaching, I encourage an environment of respect and acceptance. I appreciate the unique perspectives students bring to class, regardless of their gender, race, ethnicity or nationality, and I urge them to do likewise. In some ways, this is my way of paying forward for the support I have received in my own career.

I am a true believer that in many instances people act on stereotypes and biases just because they do not have a better understanding of the benefits of diversity, so it is important that we try to educate our colleagues and young professionals regardless of the type of work we do. Looking back at the many experiences I have had in my career in the last two decades, I can only be thankful for the many opportunities that were presented to me. I met outstanding people and had the chance to develop myself in many ways. I realized that my professional life can be satisfying by overcoming the challenges related to biases and stereotypes.

Chapter Six

Authenticity Transcends

What Stereotypes Attempt to Classify

Esther S. Gergen

Experience reveals that a journey to leadership, not unlike life's journey in general, can be lined with many detours, roadblocks and pitfalls. Many of these are presented by inheritance. Cultural and religious expectations, as well as socioeconomic conditions, are handed down from generation to generation. Yet, others are encountered in the form of gender, ethnic and age stereotypes. The latter form over many years and persist in their task of classifying people who might otherwise have many commonalities into subsets within groups and organizations based on differences. My professional success journey has indeed stumbled upon many of these inherited expectations and imposed-upon stereotypes. Neutralizing the potential effects of these on my career development has been a labor of practicing the universal value of authenticity with the exercise of leadership and calling as critical touchstones.

INHERITANCE OF CULTURE

My background as a first-generation American, Hispanic, and Generation X female is understandably ripe with opportunity for unique expectation and stereotype challenges. Born to two Mexican native parents who migrated to the United States, I came out of the womb being made painfully aware that I would have to work harder and smarter than the vast majority of my peers simply because of this beginning. Fortunately, my siblings and I had received the "smarts" gene from both our parents, who, although highly uneducated, were geniuses in their own right. Our father, born in Durango, Mexico, was pulled out of school at the age of seven to herd cattle and was therefore only able to attend school up to the first grade. I recall hearing this story as a child and being utterly confused as a teenager when he was able to assist me with my algebra homework. Determined to solve the mystery, I asked him how it was possible that he could do algebra if he only attended school up to the first grade, and he replied with a smirk, "I was a runner for engineers as a teenager and they taught me." Like I said, genius! Mom, born in Zacatecas, Mexico, was also a lover of numbers, who stopped out of her accounting program in Mexico in order to help financially support her three siblings. She could balance any books (and plates) that came her way and was particularly good at generating extra income for our family in the form of Avon sales. Hers was a modest and humble genius. I have come to realize that although my parents gifted me with intelligence, along with it, and more significantly, they also passed down to me the value of authenticity. They always knew who they were and only ever presented themselves as such, yet never allowed the assumptions of others to limit how they would accomplish success.

I was also warned about and experienced, very early in my career journey, the sting of negative assumptions about my abilities, work ethic, and dedication to the advancement of my professional achievements. Not a morning went by that Mom and Dad did not insist we make our bed as soon as we got out of it, and that we always be the first ones to arrive for school, even if the main doors of our elementary school were not yet open and we had to stand outside. "This way, everyone will know you are not lazy and really care about attending school ready to learn," they would repeatedly explain. Despite the fact that several educators along my journey had me identified as a "simple border-town girl with unrealistic ambitions," I took Mom and Dad's insistence about focusing on the substantive to heart. I set my sights on always contributing with those things I did most effectively to any and every task at hand. When high school algebra numbers made no conceptual sense, I talked myself and my friends through them with my ability to articulate concretely the abstract connections. When final exams presented an overwhelmingly impossible week of potential cramming, I used my organizational skills to create a matrix of subject modules that allowed for my study group to practice sequential review of the large amounts of information. When regional sales goals increased by 15% during a time of recession, I used my creativity to develop a new financial needs-based strategy that minimized sales intimidation for the salesforce and our clients. The priceless advice I had been given about anchoring all efforts on the substantive indeed served me well as junior class president, summa cum laude Texas A&M University graduate, MBA, regional sales leader for Citigroup, and doctoral degree recipient. It molded my belief that showing up early, working hard, and placing all efforts on identifying solutions in the face of adversity made anyone with questions associated to ethnic or gender stigmas firm believers in my ability and stamina. Plus, let's face it, who can argue with results?

GREAT EXPECTATIONS OUTSIDE THE "BUBBLE"

Along with the warnings, I had also inherited a slew of expectations about what and how Hispanic women should prioritize in the areas of family, household, faith and career. Many outsiders looking in might have described our childhood home dynamic as traditional Mexican in nature. Mom did the vast majority of the cooking, cleaning, praying and caring for us as children, while Dad worked, did all handy work around the house, and made sure we had dependable transportation. What most people did not know was that although Mom ran the household, she also worked full time at a pant factory sewing inseams on trousers. In one breath, she would say to us, "Showing love through care and nurturing is what solid women do," and in another she would say, "Women should always be able to sustain themselves financially and contribute financially to the family." Dad was just as much of a conundrum. Although his primary role was that of provider, he would quite often step in to have the puberty or peer-pressure talk, not just with the little man of the house, our brother, but also with us girls, mostly because Mom was raised to not talk about "those things." He would sit all four of us down and reiterate that he expected every one of us to obtain an education past high school, but it was just as important for us girls to learn how to cook, clean and maintain a functional household because, "No man will want a woman who cannot do these things." I recall wondering what his reaction would be to one of us girls obtaining great wealth and success and deciding we would order food in everyday because we could afford to.

It is highly relevant to emphasize that these expectations were not just unwelcome deliveries from our parents, they came from a whole tribe of grandparents, uncles, aunts, cousins and priests who felt it their community obligation to ensure I knew how I would be perceived should I deviate from expectation. "You have to use all your smarts," my grandmother would insist. "But don't make your teachers or bosses think you are smarter than them because that will cause problems." "You have the gift of understanding what motivates people, Cuz," my cousins would say, "but most of the people who you work with will probably ignore that because you are Hispanic and a woman." "God has great plans in store for you," my congregation's priest would say. "But a Godly woman's focus is always on her husband and children." Eventually, I began to identify a common thread in this pattern of "community advice." The first half of their advice always resonated with what I knew to be true about myself and the second half did not feel quite right. Additionally, and most enlightening, the advice that resonated was not associated to how I was different, but rather how I was valuable. Accordingly, I made a conscious decision to tune into what resonated and tune out what did not.

These characters and voices of limitation and expectation were not coming from a place of obstruction, but rather from a place of protection. My tribe understood that our border town of El Paso, Texas was not like most other border towns. There, we had not been marginalized throughout life for being of Mexican descent because we were, quite ironically, the majority. Most of our local store owners, entrepreneurs, bankers, priests, and teachers were just like us. The big money in El Paso, well, it had come from Northern Mexico and all of the *maquiladoras* that had generated great wealth for the owners who migrated to our town and into our neighborhoods. My graduating Bel Air High School class of 1991 was 97% Hispanic, and I only recall knowing one Black and two White fellow students.

My notion of how I would be perceived had been formed within a very unique, safe and unconventional western Texas bubble that I was about to venture out of. My tribe also understood, however, that this was not the same context I would encounter upon departing for my college and professional adventures. They knew that I would enter the halls of Texas A&M University and other parts of central and east Texas where I would indeed be the Hispanic minority. They expected that I would walk into stadium classrooms, or offices or boardrooms and be the only young Latina in the mix, and that the people already there would see primarily all of the biases and stereotypes I had yet to truly experience. But there was promise in this protective lens that I had been able to develop via my geographical context; the promise that if I remained true to universal values like hard work, organizational savvy, creativity, compassion and the desire to be valued, I might be able to represent them instead of the cultural, gender and age biases to anyone I encountered. Though a heavy burden initially, this inheritance of cultural expectations would ultimately serve as the seed that I cultivated into a voice of authenticity giving fruit to an abundance of success.

"SHEROES" WHO SHAPE US

Determined to consistently harness this voice of authenticity, I have often recalled the amazing characters who shaped my universal perspective, particularly when faced with professional leadership challenges, where others have questioned my ability to succeed. I have recalled my mother and her spirit of optimism, idealism and determination. Though she never actually spoke of these values, I could see them personified in her every day. A wife and mother of four who had no high school diploma, did not speak any English, and never learned to drive, she awoke at 5 a.m. every morning to handcraft our breakfast and lunches, and ensure her kids and husband were up, getting ready to walk to school and head out to work respectively. She would, then, proceed to carpool to the pant factory where she would sew inseams for eight hours, and communicate her consistently high production and low defect rates to a White male boss, who considered her a rock star seamstress. She would then carpool back to our home, where she would ensure that my eldest sister had started us on homework and baths so that she could cook the dinner that would get us all to sit, sharing along our stories for the day once Dad came home from work.

Many would say to her, "You really need to learn English if you want to get ahead," or "How can you continue to maintain a full-time job and care for your family without being able to drive yourself to where you need to go?" It was clear that Mom did not see the limitations and obstacles. Her optimism saw the vast opportunities that she and Dad had discovered for themselves and their children. Her idealism saw a son and three daughters who would become a future civil engineer, a furniture designer, a public-school education specialist and a college professor. Her determination fueled her desire to succeed in her seemingly mundane daily routine so that those around her could soar. She saw her struggles and obstacles as a blessing, something from which to build on, something that made her and all of us who we truly are, survivors and architects of our own success.

THE SEED OF AUTHENTICITY

Though there may have been several others before it, the first encounter with authenticity that I can recall happened at the age of eight. My parents were devout Catholics and, as such, attended mass service every Sunday with my three siblings and myself in tow. I was, distinctly enough, the only one of four children who showed any enthusiasm at the prospect of getting up at the crack of dawn to get into church digs and head over to San Antonio de Padua Catholic Church in El Paso for the 7 a.m. Spanish mass. The expectation of listening to and getting to sing along with the early service choir to those beautiful hymns had me oblivious to the fact that I could be sleeping in and rising to beans and flour tortillas instead. The early service choir at that time consisted of six singers, one acoustic guitarist and one tambourine shaker, all over the age of 50.

Though the vast majority of early-church goers might have assumed that no one was awake enough to be bothered by the minimalist nature of this choir, I found them profoundly soulful and able to personalize the meaning of those hymns just for me. I sang along to every single word of every song throughout mass, and, on one particular Sunday, Dad looked down at me and said, *"Deber í as ser parte del coro, Mija"* which was Spanish for "You should join the choir, Sweetheart." I could not think of anything else for the remainder of the service, and after the church had emptied out I walked over to the guitarist, who was also the choir leader, and announced, "I am joining your choir!" All eight members turned as if I had informed them that the Vatican was no longer endorsing the Rhythm Method, and the questions began to pour out. "But you are only eight...," "Can you sing in Spanish?" "Do you wake up this early every Sunday?" "Do your friends know you will be singing with a bunch of old people?" When the questions ceased, I simply replied, "Your music moves me and I want to be a part of doing that for other people." Shocked, amused and flattered all at the same time, they nodded to each other and the choir leader approved my admission with a "Well, ok, *nena*, we will try it." Thus began my journey towards authenticity. In that very moment, when my response touched on the universal idea of moving people through music, they no longer saw me as a child who had stumbled onto a strange curiosity, and I no longer saw them as an elite group of musically gifted older people. We were all simply lovers of hymns and their power to connect us to God. I sang at every Sunday mass service with that choir until my departure for college at the age of 18.

AUTHENTICITY TRANSFORMS

Though that had been my first experience in life with authenticity, it would not be the last time that authenticity would help me submerge age and gender stereotypes. I was fortunate enough to be entrusted with the stewardship of an entire academic department at 37—what is considered in academia a young age—and had only obtained my Ph.D. two years prior to that. The academic mentors and colleagues who had guided me through my doctoral journey saw in me the kind of leadership they were interested in experiencing for themselves, and voted unanimously to have me lead the department of Leadership Studies at Our Lady of the Lake University (OLLU) in San Antonio, Texas.

I soon discovered that the lens they saw me through did not transcend the halls of our beloved university. As I began to attend external academic administration conferences and working teams, I consistently experienced walking into rooms with all males over the age of 50. It quickly became for me a game of seeing if the next set of fellow department chairs could beat the time it would take for one of the participants to ask me, "How old are you?" Then inevitably having another say, "You are not supposed to ask women how old they are." I would casually answer, "I am in my mid-30s going on 60," and they would lightly chuckle at my clever way of letting them know that despite my age I was knowledgeable beyond my years, and that being female placed no shame on disclosing my age. Based on my previous use of authenticity to disarm stereotypes, I knew that in order for authenticity to be able to have its transcendent effects on others' biases, one has to deliver on that universal value promise. Therefore, I would immediately immerse myself in the knowledge and task at hand and become an effective part of the collective. Soon enough, the homogenous groups of middle-aged male administrators no longer saw me as a young, rookie, Hispanic, female chair and inevitably interacted with me as someone as capable and invested as they were. It turned out to be what truly mattered to us all in the end.

During this time, I became curious about what exactly my colleagues had seen in me that had led them to entrust me with leadership of the department. I asked each of them what *kind* of leadership they saw in me, and they consistently used the concepts of "real" and "genuine" to describe it. I realized that they were alluding to the same construct of authenticity that I had been encountering and utilizing throughout life, and I developed a deep desire to better know the idea of authenticity from a philosophical, intellectual and spiritual perspective. To my surprise, my curiosity led me all the way back to 18th-century English literature.

According to Canadian philosopher, Charles Taylor, the construct of authenticity is a product of the Romantic period, which took issue with disengaged rationality and an individualistic mentality that did not recognize the ties of community. Central to this view was the idea that humans are gifted with a moral understanding or internal instinct about what is right and wrong. This inherent sense of right and wrong implies that morality has an inner voice. Authenticity, then, is derived from our ability to harness morality's inner voice to be in touch with what is right to our personal inherent sense. Authenticity, thus, comes about when being in tune with our inner voice takes on autonomous and critical moral significance. It comes to exist as an indispensable requirement for the attainment of the true, full, human self.[1] Taylor's articulation of the early construction of authenticity provided, for me, the realization that being true to myself meant being steadfast about my own uniqueness, and that this uniqueness is something that *only I* can express and explore. The practice of expressing this uniqueness was the process by which I had been defining myself and enabling a potential that was suitably only mine. It was ironically, also, what had allowed me to connect with others despite the existence of perceived differences and assumptions. It was providing me a feeling of "doing my own thing," yet making me relatable to those around me, regardless of ethnic, gender or age disparities. Authenticity was the universal force that enabled others to look past my youth, ethnicity, gender and background in order to focus on what I brought forth toward the accomplishment of something mutually desired.

Though this particular explanation of authenticity had satisfied my philosophical curiosity, I was sure there had to be a spiritual aspect to the actual practice of authenticity. The idea that being in tune with our inner voice becomes of moral significance surely meant that authenticity was not an ending point itself, but rather a critical ingredient to knowing who we were placed on this earth to be. I was also left not fully understanding how exactly authenticity generated influence. I redirected my research on authenticity to the one book that I had come to know held most, if not all, of life's truths, definitions and explanations, the *Bible*. I found what I have come to believe to be the scripture's characterization of authenticity in the Book of Corinthians, specifically, Corinthians 4:3-5 in The *Christian Standard Bible* version. This passage reads,

> It is of little importance to me that I should be judged by you or by any human court. In fact, I don't even judge myself. For I am not conscious of anything against myself, but I am not justified by this. It is the Lord who judges me. So, don't judge anything prematurely, before the Lord comes, who will both bring to light what is hidden in darkness and reveal the intentions of the hearts. And then praise will come to each one from God.[2]

This spiritual application to the idea of authenticity solidified for me that the practice of authenticity requires a freedom from judgement, the judgements of others imposed on us and our own judgements imposed on others and ourselves. It requires an appreciation for our own uniqueness as well as the universal commonalities that link every one of us and inspire us to look beyond ethnicity, gender, age and socioeconomic background. God calls us to an authenticity that would allow us to both take and provide that freedom of judgement and, in doing so, harness abundant influence and success. It is through mindful practice of this type of authenticity, modeled by those before me and solidified in the teachings of the "Good Book" that I have accomplished successful leadership and today have the privilege of living out a true calling.

THE UNIVERSAL LANGUAGE OF AUTHENTIC LEADERSHIP

Leadership and calling have been two lifelong priorities for which I have worked very intentionally. Though abstract in nature, they have served well in facilitating universal connections when faced with stereotypes that would have otherwise stifled my chances at success. From a very early age, I perceived leadership to be a force or dynamic rather than a specific set of characteristics possessed by individuals. I was keenly in tune with this mysterious influence that took hold in every situation where I faced getting a group of individuals through a cumbersome challenge, problem, or decision. Though each of us in the team, as participants, were vessels that would transport our interactions from chaos to the functional accomplishment of objectives, it was this "mysterious influence" that actually did the steering through transformation. This mysterious influence transformed our deeply rooted—and often conflicting perspectives—into malleable and cohesive contributions towards collaborative results, and it fascinated me. My interest in demystifying the construct of leadership and its ability to transform led me to the pursuit of my Ph.D. in Leadership Studies, and ultimately to the work of leading with compassion and developing compassionate leadership in others. This is what I now believe I was placed in this world to do, *my calling*.

The pursuit of a doctoral degree was something that I became highly immersed in from the onset, even though I had never expected to have the chance to pursue a terminal degree. At the time that this opportunity came, I had a full-time career running credit strategy for Citigroup, a husband, a seven-year-old boy, and very busy household to manage. Just about the only space available in my week was on the weekend, and the Leadership Studies doctoral program at OLLU offered just that, weekend classes. Upon discussing the opportunity with my Human Resources manager, I additionally learned that Citigroup would provide 80% tuition reimbursement if I decided to enroll.

Though I knew it would require my family and home to sacrifice some of the limited time I had with them, I tuned into that inner voice that kept telling me that opportunities like these are hard to come by. Today, when I am asked how I was able to obtain a doctoral degree while practicing a career in banking and managing a household, I seldom speak of how daunting the challenge seemed or how unlikely it would be for a first-generation Latina post-graduate student to actually complete the degree. Instead, I explain that the financial and time opportunities aligned so closely to what was in my heart about the next phase of my intellectual and academic growth that I could not possibly allow them to pass me by. This lesson in authenticity is simple, if we are to access the power of universal values to break down ethnic, gender, age and cultural stereotypes, we must empower ourselves with every opportunity that aligns closely to our dreams and ambitions.

In the Leadership Studies doctoral program, I came to discover that leadership in and of itself is indeed a process or dynamic, and, as such, is ever fluid and conceptualized in many vastly diverse ways. I learned that leadership can come to life in a set of traits such as determination, integrity and sociability. It can develop via interactions, behaviors and relationships within a group of individuals. It can even happen in various styles of influence from inspiration, and motivation to coercion and transaction. The scholarly understanding of leadership has magnified my ability to put it into practice 10 times over, and has gifted me with the validation that authenticity does indeed have a vital role in the formation of effective leadership. Even more, it has verified that there is a genuine quality in the right kind of leadership that can transcend stereotypes, and this verification came through the work of

American businessman and academic, Bill George, who introduced the construct of Authentic Leadership.[3]

According to George, authentic leaders demonstrate a passion for their purpose, practice their values steadfastly, and lead with their hearts as well as their minds. They develop long-lasting meaningful relationships and have the discipline to get results. Primarily, however, they know who they are and remain true to themselves. A real conceptual model of what I know to be the driving force for how I approach success despite barriers does indeed exist, and I had traveled the journey to it just as described by its author. The journey to Authentic Leadership, according to George, begins with comprehending the narrative of your life. Your life narrative affords the texture for your experiences and through it you discover the inspiration to have an effect in the world. Your life narrative is significant because it provides the very substance that plays in your mind when you tune in to that inner voice which in turn enables you to center your approach to challenges, decisions and interactions on your true self.[4] The authenticity that I have derived from practicing universal values, tuning into my life narrative, and knowing who I am have continuously and consistently enabled me to deploy a type of connection with others that has gone beyond and broken through the barriers of classification and bias which I have encountered throughout my leadership journey.

THE TRANSCENDENT EFFECT

Success in leadership has not been accomplished by my efforts alone. Identifying the value of authenticity in others has also played a key role in my ability to overcome paradigms that attempted to limit my potential. Throughout my corporate and academic career, I have been surrounded by individuals who live out their values every day, and who have invested of their time and attention toward mentoring me and enabling me to grow and succeed. Often, however, other people's personal truths do not align to ours, but that does not make them any less authentic than our own. Others are also building leadership and success from completely different life narratives. Being able to recognize, appreciate, and delicately navigate through the differences within each individual's inner voice is essential to practicing *personal* authenticity and reaching *personal* success without stifling the authenticity of others who are on their own leadership and success journey.

For instance, the first movement for gender equality in financial compensation that I embarked on was *my very own* personal one, and an example of how recognizing that authenticity comes in many forms serves the ultimate accomplishment of a principle objective. I highlight the concept of principle because financial compensation has never been a primary motivator for why and how I exercise my calling. Despite that, there came a time early in my administrative assignment as an academic department chair that I began to inquire about differences in financial compensation among department chairs in the school within which my department was housed. I had observed through "water cooler" conversation with my fellow peers that male department chairs were being financially compensated at a significantly higher percentage than female chairs. The ever optimist in me thought it might have to do with academic discipline rather than with gender, but I decided to inquire nonetheless. In a meeting with my dean at the time, who was a White male in his mid-50s, I informed him that I had come to the knowledge that a couple of the male department chairs with relatively similar tenure as myself were being paid at least $10 thousand more per year than I was. I calmly awaited that he would confirm that it had to do with academic discipline, but much to my disappointment he informed me that the male department chairs were the main sources of income for their families, and, as such, required more compensation. He also encouraged me to be patient because he saw in me the potential to be an executive administrator for our university one day.

Rather than succumbing to the slow building of outrage I had begun to feel, I decided instead to ask if he would share his personal journey to dean. He openly proceeded to share with me that he had been in the military early in his life and had obtained his bachelors, master's, and doctoral degrees while balancing a family and career. He had done this as the sole financial provider for his family, which required sacrifice, but more importantly the ability to make an adequate salary with which to do so. In that moment, I understood that his paradigm and response came from *his* life's narrative, and, although it may have felt inadequate to me, it was his personal truth and it had garnished him success thus far. I thanked him for sharing his story with me and walked out of his office unsuccessful in obtaining an equitable level of pay for myself. Although understanding my dean's personal truth provided little comfort to being unable to correct the pay inequity, I somehow appreciated that he expressed his vision of my potential, and it gave me a sense of resolve that his inadequate paradigm came not from a malignant place, but rather from being authentic and loyal to his own inner voice. I also knew in my heart that another opportunity would present itself eventually that might have the authenticity stars better aligned.

That opportunity indeed came when a new dean was assigned to the leadership of our school. The university had ventured into diversifying the administrative roles across academic units and hired an African American economist originally from California, but who was very traveled and diverse in his professional experience. I immediately identified with him through initial interactions that he did not define himself by his ethnicity or background, and he based his judgements about the various academic departments solely on the quality of the work and contributions occurring in each respective area. It was also evident that he understood early on that our department was accomplishing great success with a relatively limited amount of resources. Our department had just recently hired two additional full-time faculty members and the financial compensation of the new male faculty member had been set by the previous dean. This compensation also happened to be several thousand dollars higher than my own as department chair.

Sensing that the stars might be aligning, I took the opportunity during one of our planning sessions to surface my observation about the disparity in pay between myself as chair and the newly hired faculty member. He instantly stated, "What do you mean; what is your currently salary?" Upon receiving my salary amount, he did not further inquire about the new faculty member's past experience, previous tenure, gender or age; he simply stated, "I will make it a priority to fix this." Remaining steadfast to my approach, I proceeded to ask if he would share his personal journey to dean. As openly as my previous dean had, he proceeded to share that he had also served in the military early in his career and had obtained his bachelor's, master's and doctoral degrees while balancing a marriage and career. He also shared with me that he had encountered many instances in which he was offered opportunities—both financial and professional—solely based on the fact that he was a Black male. He emphasized that he turned many of them down because he wanted to be rewarded only for the contributions that his abilities and hard work had generated. He also had a life narrative that formed his paradigms and response to the compensation disparity, which happened to be aligned with my own. Two weeks later, I received an updated contract detailing my new salary, which had been increased by several thousand dollars.

Though many might read the last two experiences of my personal movement toward financial compensation equality and interpret the theme to be that one has to wait for the right-minded person to come along and enable one's success—financial or otherwise—my hope is that a completely different and transcending theme emerges; the theme that although our own authenticity has great influence on our ability to generate effective leadership and success in the face of biases and stereotypes, authenticity of those with whom we share work, career and a calling is just as powerful. When we unleash our own authenticity and honor that those around us must unleash their own unique brand of authenticity, the cumulative success grows exponentially and the effects of cultural, ethnic, gender and age biases are all but eliminated.

If I had to anchor my description of how I have been able to silence biases in leadership on one specific statement, I would choose the words of the great Maya Angelou. Angelou has brilliantly shared her perspective on the power of female authenticity in the following quote, "A woman in harmony with her spirit is like a river flowing. She goes where she will without pretense and arrives at her destination prepared to be herself and only herself."[5] I interpret this to mean that our spirits are the metaphysical representation of our true selves and as such have no gender, culture or ethnic limitations by which to be classified or judged. The authenticity of our spirits elevates us and all whom we encounter to a level of consciousness where our individual differences seize to exist and are replaced by common universal values. I believe that herein lies the power of our authentic selves to transcend and overcome the expectations and stereotypes we have faced and will continue to face both personally and professionally. Herein also lies my personal vision around the kind of woman, leader and professional I strive to be.

NOTES

1. Taylor, C. (1992). *The ethics of authenticity.* Cambridge, MA: Harvard University Press

2. Holman Bible Publishers (2017). *The Christian Standard Bible*, 1 Corinthians 4:3–6.

3. George, B. (2003). *Authentic leadership: Rediscovering the secrets to creating lasting value.* San Francisco, Calif.: Jossey-Bass.

4. George, B. (2003). *Authentic leadership: Rediscovering the secrets to creating lasting value.* San Francisco, Calif.: Jossey-Bass.

5. Quote Ambition. (2018). *75 Maya Angelou quotes on love, life, courage, and women.* Retrieved from http://www.quoteambition.com/maya-angelou-quotes-love-life-courage-women/

Chapter Seven

Fluid Identities

How Growing Up in a Lower-class Brazilian Immigrant Family Shaped My Ideas of Class, Race, and Culture

Damaris Santos Palmer

HUMBLE BEGINNINGS

I was born in the 1980s in Sao Paulo, Brazil, in a period when the country was going through vast political transformations from a military dictatorship to a democracy. My parents, both holding technical high-school diplomas, were in their early 20s when they had me during a time when my mother was a preschool teacher and my father was an art teacher. My mother was happy living close to her own mother and siblings, raising my sister and I around our extended family. She also enjoyed her job, her friends, and her community, but my father was a misfit and struggled with his identity as he had been addicted to drugs in his teens and had no hope for the future.

One day, however, at a train station in Sao Paulo, my father connected with a young American expatriate who had served a Mormon mission in Brazil, and, similarly to the transformations happening in the country, my family was also about to go through great changes. As my father and this young man became friends, he left behind a life of drugs, finding a new community within the Mormon church. Because of his dramatic conversion, my father transferred the energy of his old habits into his new religion, and, in a way, he became addicted to religion. On one hand, my father was extremely creative and free-spirited, but on the other hand—the side that always prevailed—he was very strict; he tried to set up a clear life structure, and he devoted himself to a religion that, especially at that time, was very patriarchal and White-American centric. In his journey through this new lifestyle, my father left to the United States on his own with a goal of one day moving us all to Salt Lake City, Utah, so that we could be closer to the headquarters of the Mormon church.

In 1990, the day before my seventh birthday, my mother, my sister and I moved to the U.S. to be reunited with my father. My mother was devastated to leave her family and her career behind, but my father—as the patriarch of the family—led the way. At that time, his only contact in the U.S. was a Brazilian high school friend who lived in Chicago, and who had recently received his American residency when Ronald Reagan signed The Immigration Reform and Control Act of 1986,[1] granting amnesty to millions of undocumented immigrants. My father, as were many others, was hopeful that amnesty would happen again, but it never did, so for six years we lived in Chicago, fearful of being caught and being deported. To pay the bills, my father drove a cab and my mother worked both as a nanny and house cleaner; and with the limited financial resources, my father's dream of moving to Salt Lake City in order to live in a predominantly Mormon community never came true. Instead, we lived in a diverse immigrant neighborhood and went to an inner-city public school with very little resources, much to my father's dismay.

In the early 1990s, there were not many Brazilian immigrants in Chicago, so when my sister and I started attending our neighborhood public school, since we only knew how to speak Portuguese, we were placed in an English-as-a-Second Language (ESL) class, where all the other students spoke Spanish. My mother advocated for us and told the school that she wanted us to be in mainstream classes, but the school administrators kept us with the other immigrants, and they also made me repeat first grade since I had moved from Brazil in the middle of the American school year and did not speak any English. Once school was out, my sister and I went to our neighborhood's Boys and Girls Club every day because my parents had to work long hours.

Most of the kids in this afterschool program spoke Spanish, so I started to pick up Spanish and English at the same time. However, the neighborhood was very segregated between Mexicans and Puerto Ricans, and even at the Boys and Girls Club kids tended to divide themselves depending on where they were originally from, but since I was not part of either group, it was very confusing to my fellow first graders and to myself that I was neither Mexican nor Puerto Rican. I remember a particular experience that year when I was at the playground trying to play with some children, and a third grader said, "Hey, you just have to choose! Do you want to be Mexican or do you want to be Puerto Rican?" The Mexican kids went to one side of the playground, the Puerto Ricans to the other side, and I was literally left in the middle of the playground with this bossy third grader who was forcing me to pick a side. Looking around, I saw four White kids on top of the slide, so I asked, "Can I just go with them?" The children all laughed, and without understanding what was happening, I felt stuck, and in a hasty decision I chose to stick with the Puerto Rican kids.

That night, when I was retelling my family what had happened, my father became disappointed, and told me, "You are *not* Hispanic, do you understand? You are White! Your skin is White. Hispanics speak Spanish and we speak Portuguese," as he tried very hard to assimilate and to be accepted into the White American culture. We joined a church congregation that was far away from our house just so we could integrate with White Americans. My mother, on the other hand, socialized with the other nannies who were mostly immigrants and Latinas, and she respected these ladies who helped her find her way across a new city. She was much less worried about assimilating into White culture, and she saw Latina immigrants as allies, not as threats, and definitely not as inferior to her.

Although we were all living this new life together, my parents coped in different ways. They were immigrants in a new country where they did not speak the language, in a time where the internet was not available, and there was little opportunity to remain connected to family back in our native Brazil. My father resented other immigrants and was offended that he was seen as Hispanic, while my mother embraced it as a means of social support, which caused a lot of tension in their marriage. In addition to this stress on my parents' relationship, things were not easy with us children either, so after two unsuccessful years in public school, and receiving no help from the administrators, my mother decided to transfer me and my sister to a bilingual magnet school, where my mother's English teacher worked. My father only agreed to this switch because the new school was in a nice, affluent neighborhood of Chicago.

FINDING SUPPORT AND FIGHTING FOR RIGHTS

This school was a game changer, where Mexican, Puerto Rican, Central American, African American, and Caucasian students all learned Spanish. The teachers did an exceptional job at celebrating different cultures, and one of my teachers learned about an exhibit in the Children's Museum in Madison, Wisconsin, which was going to showcase Brazilian culture. He and his wife drove me and my sister three hours away just so we could see this display, instilling in me that cultural representation mattered. This teacher was willing to sacrifice his Saturday, his gas, and his money to give me and my sister an experience where we were able to see our Brazilian culture in a museum.

I am so grateful for this teacher and the other educators I had at that school. In the four years I attended this bilingual elementary school, I learned Spanish, I was given the help I needed to thrive academically, and I was also taught a lot about social justice when my teachers took us to rallies to advocate for immigrant rights. During that time, I remember a lot of discussion about free and reduced lunch for undocumented children, and one of my teachers marched up on stage during the Republican National Convention, approached the microphone and screamed something about free and reduced lunch for *all* children regardless of their legal status, but next time we saw him three days later, it was at his court hearing. Looking back, I am so grateful for the tenacity of these educators to put a group of rowdy children on a train, take us downtown Chicago, and teach us about civics in action. Their activism both inside and outside of the classroom shaped so much of who I am today. However, protesting was not all we learned. At school, we read literature from authors of color both male and female, we saw pictures on the classroom walls—down to the clipart—that were thought out and represented children with various skin tones, and we had social functions where families could gather and eat foods from different countries and cultures. School was now an incredible place where I always felt safe.

However, after six years of living undocumented in Chicago, my parents started growing more and more fearful and they realized that the opportunities for me and my sister to be fully integrated into society would be extremely difficult. My parents also feared family separation. After we had been in the U.S. for two years, my mother had given birth to my youngest sister, and though she brought so much joy to our home, she also created constant fear for my parents because, if we were to one day be deported, she—as an American citizen—would have to stay behind and be placed in foster care. So, in 1996, my parents decided to pack everything and move our family back to Sao Paulo, Brazil.

COMING "HOME"

I had spent my formative years in Chicago without having had much contact with my extended family. I spoke Portuguese, but now I had an accent, and all of my education had been in English and Spanish. The only music I knew in Portuguese was what my parents had introduced me to, which was definitely not what my cousins or any of the kids my age were listening to, and I also did not know anything about current pop culture in Brazil, so I immediately felt like an outsider when I went back "home." I did not feel very Brazilian, but I also could not claim that I was American, and I experienced a huge dichotomy of ethnic cultural identity.

As we started getting settled into our new life, my parents enrolled me in public school, but it was nothing like the public school I had attended in Chicago. In Brazil, there were 48 kids in my seventh grade homeroom, and we did not even have enough desks for all of us to sit. Also, there was no school library, and there were barely any textbooks in the school at all. At the same time that I longed for my education back in Chicago, I also made wonderful friends in my new school. Teachers often did not show up to class, so there was a lot of time for socializing, playing soccer, listening to music and learning new dances, and I quickly fell in love with my new friends and this fun, upbeat culture I was being reintroduced to.

When I finished middle school, I wanted to challenge myself and get a better education. Public school, unfortunately, was not going to cut it, and I knew that I would not be able to meet my goal of eventually moving back to the U.S. for college on a full ride scholarship since my family had no money. I tried to obtain financial assistance at various different private schools throughout the city, but the best offer I received was partial tuition aid. Then, one day, I met the Sao Paulo Mormon Mission President's wife, who was American, and she changed my life. In a quick and casual conversation, I introduced myself told her, in a nutshell told her about my time in Chicago, and asked her if she had any books I could borrow since I had already read and reread several times all of the English books I had brought back to Brazil with me. She had a daughter my age and told me she would help me get more books.

Her daughter was a student at the prestigious American school in Sao Paulo, a high-end private school for mostly expatriate children whose parents are transferred to Brazil for work—CEOs and other executives of large corporations, diplomats, ambassadors, and prominent religious leaders, or very wealthy Brazilians who can afford the high tuition cost. This American woman serving the Mormon church at the time helped me with much more than English books to read. Thanks to her very generous effort, and the quick response from my teachers back in Chicago who wrote letters of recommendation and submitted my test scores and transcripts, I was awarded a full scholarship to this American high school in Sao Paulo, and I am certain that having had access to this first-class education changed my life.

Although I was exhilarated with this opportunity, I encountered several difficulties, too, of course. First, it took me three hours each way to get from my house to school by public transportation, so after a couple of weeks of making the daily trek, my parents decided it was best to rent a room near the school for me to stay during the week. I was only 14 years old, starting high school in a new and very rigorous school, I had very little money, and I lived away from my family during the week. In order to help pay for my room and board, and to start saving money to take the Scholastic Assessment Test (SAT) which would be required for my college applications, I worked evenings and summers teaching English to executives. This was my introduction to the workforce.

The school where I worked was owned and run by two go-getter women, whom, as a young teenager, I considered to be role models. I was still 14 years old when I started teaching adult students, and, being so young, I did not realize it then, but I was a target in numerous sexual harassment situations. I had barely received any training from my employers, but I did not care because I was a confident teenager who really needed money, I was very disciplined, had good work ethic, and spoke fluent English. The school owners trusted me to do my best work and, in return, I trusted them that they knew what was best for me. During the four years I taught English—the entire time while being underage—all of my students were men, except for one. Their companies were paying for them to learn English, and it was often apparent that they were not necessarily there by choice, but because it was an obligation. Frequently, my male students would excuse their inappropriate behavior, justifying that they were just *practicing* English. They would say, "Teacher, you look so hot today," "*Professora*, is it grammatically correct if I say . . . [insert something about sex]?" And if the students noticed that I was uncomfortable, they would just laugh.

However, one of the last students I had was a young entrepreneur, the owner of a bookstore chain in Brazil. Unlike the other students I had, who had little regard for my time, often being late or absent, this male student was always on time, never canceled class and was very engaged in the lessons. One time, I made the observation to him that it was so refreshing to have a student who was actually excited about learning English, and that a lot of my other students just wanted to goof off. He was always very respectful and focused on the classes, and his overall behavior was different as he never made any comments about how I looked or anything of sexual nature. I brought this up to my supervisors, and asked if they could please assign me more students like this one. Their attitude was simply one of "What do you expect? This is Brazil and this is how men behave here, especially men of power. You are just too young to understand, but get used to it." After years of teaching and putting up with sexual harassment from my students, it took *one* man who acted respectfully for me to understand that what I had experienced from the other students was not okay. I told my supervisors that I would continue teaching the one student who was respectful, but that I wanted nothing more with the other students; a very difficult decision to make since I was a senior in high school trying to earn money to pay for the college application exams, as well as attempting to save money to attend a university in the U.S.

In the evenings when I was not teaching English, I was busy keeping up with my school work. I was in a rigorous International Baccalaureate (I.B.) program, I had been elected student council president, I was in the National Honor Society (NHS), while maintaining a straight-A transcript. My school was very rigorous and gave me access to so many opportunities, from incredible facilities to highly educated and trained teachers, to a dedicated college counselor, who helped me every step of the way so that I could come back to the U.S. to attend a university. In September of my senior year, the month when I started applying for colleges in the U.S., I was sitting in my I.B. History class, reading *A People's History of the United States* by Howard Zinn,[2] when my college counselor walked in and told the teacher to turn on the television because a plane had hit one of the World Trade Center buildings in New York City.[3] We watched in horror as the event unfolded, and, from that moment on, there was a wave of uncertainty, including rumors that immigration laws would change for international student visas and that universities would no longer accept international students. Even amidst all the unknown, I applied to over 20 colleges, hoping that I would receive enough financial aid to at least one of them.

FOLLOWING MY DREAMS

In spring of 2002, shortly after my 19th birthday, I received the news that I had been accepted to Mount Holyoke College, and received a very generous scholarship. My dream of returning to the U.S. was coming true! At home, though, things were tumultuous. My parents were going through a divorce, my 21-year-old sister had become a single mother, and financially we were even more strapped than ever before. I felt guilty about leaving my family and did not even know how I would be able to afford my airfare. However, even with everything that was going on in my personal life, I graduated from high school with high honors, as one of the top 10 students in my graduating class, and qualified for a scholarship from the school's Parent Teacher Association (PTA) for community service, which was generous enough for me to pay my enrollment fees at Mount Holyoke College. Then, a very generous member of my church congregation gave me an airplane ticket to Chicago, where I would spend the summer babysitting for a family we had met several years earlier. Everything fell into place and I left my family and friends behind, and set out for college.

After spending the summer working in Chicago, I flew out to Newark, New Jersey. This was my first time ever on the East Coast, and everything felt so new! After landing, I took a train to Springfield, Massachusetts, and I just remember everything being so expensive. I got to Mount Holyoke College with a couple of hundred dollars in my pocket. I had missed the bus from Springfield to the college and ended up having to pay for a cab, and, to make it worse, by the time I arrived on campus, I had missed dinner. I knew that I would have to buy books, all my personal care items plus come up with $800 a semester to pay the "parental contribution" portion of my tuition, which my parents had no way of paying. As an international student, I knew that I would have limited opportunities for employment on campus and I had no idea how much money I would actually make. All of those thoughts were crossing my mind when I got to campus for the first time. Years later, for my 10-year reunion, I returned to campus and was really emotional remembering the first time I had stepped foot on that beautiful, historic campus, and how—instead of feeling victorious for having been accepted there, or rather than being in awe of the beauty of the place—I felt hungry, worried, and so tired of being poor. I was very worried about money, so instead of going across the street that first night to buy myself some food, I decided to just go to bed hungry.

That was not the only time that I had to decide between eating a meal or saving money for books. When Thanksgiving rolled around, all of the dining halls were going to shut down for the extended weekend. Most of the students went home or to relatives' houses for the holiday, but the majority of the international students stayed behind. We were an interesting mix; there were some international students who, like myself, were at Mount Holyoke thanks to financial aid, while others were very wealthy, and could afford to travel somewhere fun. As part of the first group, I was stuck on campus. Several of us were very worried about how we would get food those days; we were nearing the end of the semester and our funds were low. We did not have money to eat out and we did not want to spend our money buying groceries, especially because we only had access to a microwave and a mini fridge.

All first-year international students employed on campus worked in the dining halls, the only work-study option we had. Wednesday before Thanksgiving, as we were cleaning out the dining hall, I asked the cook if I could please grab the sandwiches they were throwing away for myself and some of my friends who would be on campus for the four-day weekend. The cook told me that she could not allow it, and that all the food needed to be thrown away as the school had to abide by national Food Safety Regulations, and that was one of the rules. That same evening, the cook called me and said, "Hey, Damaris, I'm really not supposed to do this, but I put a trash bag with some food for you and the other girls next to the trashcan; I didn't put it inside it. Come grab what you need. Happy Thanksgiving!" Thanks to this cafeteria cook we had grab-and-go sandwiches, salads, juices, chips, and apples to tide us over for the next few days until the cafeterias opened again. It is a very unique experience to be a part of an institution that is so affluent when you are so not. Since I was such a minority in the institution, I noticed that administrators did not understand most of our struggles. I definitely felt supported academically, though, and am so grateful for the generosity of the school in awarding me financial aid, but there were day-to-day circumstances—including not being able to call home to talk to family—I had to endure that are already difficult when you are poor, but become especially arduous when you are an international student.

Through such experiences and many others, I found that Mount Holyoke was a microcosm of what I would experience later in life outside of college, especially in regards to race. The first week of school during orientations, I attended an icebreaker activity with my roommate, an Asian American young woman. We had arrived a little late and had missed the instructions, so the older students who were leading the activity invited my friend and I to sit inside the circle with a group of other students. Outside of the circle there was another group of students sitting in a bigger circle around us. This activity was called fishbowl, and its objective was to encouraged us to listen to others' experiences. The group on the outside had to write anonymous questions on a piece of paper and then put them inside a fishbowl. The group on the inside, then, would draw a paper with a question and discuss the answer, while the group on the outside would listen respectfully without interrupting. It can be a very powerful activity. Since my roommate and I were late, I did not know exactly what we were doing, but it was there and then that I was introduced to the term "women of color," and that was when I found out that in America people viewed *me* as a woman of color. In my early years in Chicago, we never referred to anyone as being "of color."

In my former American schools, one was either Hispanic, Black, or White, and ever since that moment in the playground when I was seven years old and had to pick a side between Mexicans and Puerto Ricans, I had a very difficult time identifying with any group other than Brazilian. Then, when I was in Brazil, I was considered White. When I went to college, I saw myself as an international student and that was all I thought I was. But, that day during orientation, I realized that in America I was also considered a woman of color. It felt like such a huge weight had been put on my shoulders. All of a sudden, the group on the outside was expecting me to share experiences of how hard it was to be a woman of color, but I did not have any of the same experiences that the other women with this label in the circle had had. They were African American women and Latinas, who had been born and raised in the U.S., and had been racially marginalized their whole lives. I had been living in Brazil for the past six years, where I was seen as a White, and I had never experienced any racial discrimination in my country, where I understood so much more about class divide rather than racial segregation. I felt like, all of a sudden, I had a responsibility to understand the experiences of women of color in the U.S., and that, if I was going to be seen as one, I needed to understand the history of struggle and resistance that women of color in the U.S. had endured.

This early experience back in the U.S. brought me awareness to the cultural differences I would encounter. I felt like I had won the lottery as far as academic experiences were concerned; I had incredibly dedicated professors and was empowered by being a part of an all-women's college. I met bright, intelligent, women who have gone on to do wonderful things with their lives.

During my years at Mount Holyoke, I took full advantage of the academic opportunities that I had. I also made wonderful friends, worked as a resident advisor, and joined volunteer clubs, as well as politically driven groups. At the time, as a very active member of the Mormon church, during freshman year, I met my husband at a church social function. He was American, but had served a Mormon mission in Brazil and spoke fluent Portuguese, and was enrolled in a master's degree program in Environmental Sciences at Yale University. While I was preparing for an internship with a Non-governmental Organization (NGO) that promoted sustainable development in Brazil, he was getting ready to work on his master's thesis research in Acre, Brazil, studying rubber tappers in the Amazon and how they implemented sustainable development practices. We had a lot to talk about; our interest and passion for social justice was definitely the catalyst of our relationship. In the summer of my sophomore year, when I was only 21 years old, we got married.

WHAT'S NEXT?

My husband graduated with his master's degree from Yale a week before we were married, so we returned to Massachusetts after our wedding for me to finish school. Some women in my church congregation were surprised that my husband would move to a small town in western Massachusetts so that I could finish college instead of me just dropping out of school to follow him somewhere else where he could find a better job. Luckily for me, my husband and I saw eye-to-eye on this issue; we were a team and we would support each other. We made a very conscious decision early in our marriage that we would not abide by strict gender roles, especially the ones we were often prescribed by members of our church, and that we would be supportive of each other's careers. However, to be honest, this was easier said than done; not because my husband wavered, but because *I did*. I felt a lot of pressure and guilt, especially when I had my first child. My husband's extended family expected me to be a stay-at-home mom, and all of my sisters-in-law at the time were homemakers. My local church leaders were also encouraging women to stay home, and so were my church sisters, who stayed home with their children.

I did not feel that staying home forever would be right for me, so I made sure to complete my studies, and I graduated from college with a two-month-old baby. Soon after, we moved to Hawaii, where my husband had been raised, to be closer to his family and to, hopefully, have him find a job, so at that time, giving into my family and religious cultural pressures, I decided that I was going to be a stay-at-home mom. However, after a short couple of months, I fell into depression. I was miserable! I lived in a small Mormon town, where my circle of friends were all homemakers and non-professionals. I had gone from having heated inspiring discussions about political issues with my college friends to having passionate conversations about what brand of baby wipes was best. I saw that many of my friends loved the mom life; they loved staying home with their children and all the day-to-day activities of managing a household. I longed for that feeling; I prayed to have those feelings, but I never did. Instead, I *resented* my new role so much!

My husband could see that I was miserable. He was working a couple of part-time jobs and was not having any luck finding permanent positions, so we both decided to apply to graduate school. So, soon after a year of arriving in Hawaii, we left to start a new adventure in California with a young child in tow. In the fall of 2007, I started a master's program and my husband started a doctorate. We lived on campus in student family housing, and I was ecstatic to be back on a college campus. My husband and I coordinated our schedules so that we could co-parent our son equally, and the whole time I was in graduate school, our son was home with us. The one daycare on campus had a huge waitlist and our boy never got to enroll. This experience really set the roots for how my husband and I would parent our son, and then later on our other two children. We were forced to learn to communicate a lot, and hold weekly planning sessions so that we could both get our school work done, do our teaching assistant (TA) jobs, spend quality time with our son, and manage our overall household. My husband took charge of the cleaning and I took charge of the cooking. We both earned the same amount of money and we both spent the same amount of time with our son; we were on an equal playing fields where we got to evaluate our strengths and our weaknesses and make compromises and adjustments so that we could run our household in an egalitarian manner. And this made me so much happier than living the life of a stay-at-home mom as I felt I could be myself.

After I finished my master's degree, I gave birth to our second child. During that time, I continued to work as a TA, and I started spending a lot of time blogging and growing that platform as a business. Meanwhile, my husband and I continued to divide up the household and parenting duties, making changes when needed to adapt. This was a hectic time, but also a really exciting point in my life. I loved blogging! It reminded me so much of my time at Mount Holyoke College when I had the opportunity to exercise my mind. Blogging, I found a community of women who were outspoken like me and where becoming online influencers, and I was very curious as to how these women, many of whom were stay-at-home Mormon moms were making a living from their blog. So, I attended blogging conferences, participated in online forums, read other blogs and kept up with my own online writing; I wrote sponsored posts for clients and networked with other bloggers to collaborate on paid projects. I loved the idea that I could make money, build an online content business, and work from home.

A few years later, in the summer of 2011, my husband and I set out to Bahia, Brazil, with our two young kids. He was going to work on his doctoral research and I would continue blogging from Brazil, doing what I loved and earning an income. During our stay in Brazil, we decided to have another child and I became pregnant with our third child, and, this time, I was very sick, I was on bed rest for several weeks of my pregnancy, and I had very little stamina to continue blogging. I really worried that my blog would lose steam and that I would have to start it all over again. But, in the summer of 2012, after spending a year in Brazil, I returned to the U.S. with the two little children and the third one on the way. I was finally starting to feel better, and one of the media agencies for which I had written some sponsored content had recently opened a temporary position, so I applied for the job as content manager and was so very happy when I was selected for the job. My husband was still in Brazil finishing up his research, so I moved in with his grand-mother and aunt, who watched my children for me to commute an hour and a half to two hours each day to San Francisco.

This was a huge sacrifice for our family, but I wanted to get my shoe in the door, and I needed to keep my mind active to stay healthy. I loved blogging, but I was getting burnt out from content creation and from keeping up with social media, so since I was always interested in the *business* of blogging, this was my chance to be on the other side of the table, and learn the intricacies of how the industry worked. Although things were fine, it was very difficult to carry on with the commute, the job, and the children, so my husband returned from Brazil a couple weeks earlier than expected to help with the children. He was excited for me about my new job, and he knew that it was something that I was passionate about, so he whole-heartedly supported me. After a short three months, my temporary contract ended, a week later my third child was born, and a month after her birth the same company offered me a full-time position as editor and content manager. We were busy, but this is what I wanted to do, so I accepted the job with my husband's full support.

For the next three years, I worked at this large media company. We were an amazing team; and out of the eight editors and content managers seven were women, which was great since the majority our bloggers were women. However, I noticed that most the staff in the Sales and Marketing departments were male, as well as most of the executives at the organization. Fortunately, I felt like our opinions as women were valued and held in high regard; most of our content creators were also women and we knew what kind of content would sell, or what kind of material would be a bust. We knew what messages would pick up engagement, and which would not. And, even though the higher positions at the company were staffed by men, because the Sales team and Marketing group were good about taking our opinions as editors into consideration, I felt like I mattered.

After six months of working for this company, I received a promotion. I pitched a new content program and my idea came into fruition, so I was asked to spearhead this program. At the time I had an infant, a toddler, and a child in the first grade, and, before the new position, I would commute an hour and half from Santa Cruz to San Francisco only twice a week. The rest of the time, I worked from home. My husband stayed with our children, and, during the hours he was in class, we hired a babysitter. The promotion was an incredible opportunity for me and my family, and, with the help of my mentor who coached me to negotiate my salary—the woman who first hired me but was no longer working for this company—I was going to be making very good money. However, the new job required me to be in the office every day, and since I was still nursing the baby and waking up multiple times in the middle of the night, we decided to leave Santa Cruz and make our way up to San Francisco so I would not have to commute.

I took on this new role and had a lot of encouragement from my husband. At the time, he was finishing his doctoral dissertation and he spent his days as full-time lead parent, taking care of the house, and at nights, when I got home, he would retreat and work on writing his dissertation. After only seven months of living in San Francisco, my husband was offered a full-time position working as a professor in Hawaii. He was so happy! He had always wanted to move back to Hawaii and work in the state where he had grown up. I, however, was less thrilled. My first experience living in Hawaii a few years back had not been great, but I needed to be as supportive of him as he had been of me, so I spoke with my supervisors and was very surprised when they allowed me to keep my position and work remotely. So, in the summer of 2014, we moved our family back to the rainbow state.

Working from home, so far away from the office, proved to be a huge challenge. I had to work Pacific Standard Time, which meant that for half of the year my workday started at 6 a.m. in my local time zone. I bought into the idea that this would be my chance to do it all; I could work eight hours a day from 6 a.m. to 2 p.m., then I could pick up my son from school and my daughters from the babysitter's at 2:15 p.m. and turn into "Super Mom." My husband was starting his career in academia and had a daily commute of 45 minutes each way. For the first time in our lives as parents, we were both working full time and he was much less available at home. When we were in California, I had been working full time in San Francisco, but had a stay-at-home spouse who took care of the kids and of the household. Now, my husband was at work from 8 a.m. to 5 p.m., some days even longer, and stressed about starting his new demanding career. Meanwhile, my job was gaining steam and I was successfully growing my team remotely, but working nine-hour days was not cutting it. I logged off the computer at 2 p.m., rushed out of the house to pick up the children, and immediately logged back on to answer emails and other messages. After the children's bedtime, I jumped back online and worked for a couple more hours just to be up at 5:30 a.m. the next morning, and start it all over again.

Both my husband and I were vigorously working full time, and I did not have any sort of break—not even a commute where I could unwind. I worked from home, and then, after work, I was home with three children trying to feed them, clean, do homework, and parent until my husband was home from work. However, even when he was home, he was also often busy preparing for his next class or getting ready for upcoming faculty meetings. This schedule was not sustainable and my health had started to suffer. I never had time to exercise, I sat at a desk 12 hours a day, I rarely ate a real meal, and I was very stressed. I am not sure if I would have had the physical and mental capacity to continue working as much as I had been. However, I could also not imagine that I would have ever quit my job. After all, I loved it!

Following a year and a half of this chaotic lifestyle, I was told that I no longer could work remotely. At the time, I interpreted this as a tragedy, but now I see it as luck. At first, we had even considered returning to California so that I could keep my job, but my children were thriving in Hawaii. And, as my husband and I stopped to think about our family, we realized that if I continued working the way I had been, my health would probably get worse and worse, so, *together*, we decided that we were going to stay in Hawaii and figure out what came next. And, as if this had been the plan all along, a month after leaving that job, I found another position doing similar work for a much smaller media company. During the weeks I had between jobs, I got caught up on sleep, started exercising, ate better and felt incredible overall. I knew that I did not want to be a full-time homemaker, but I also could not work 12-hour days much longer. So, accepting that sometimes we just have to slow down, I have found life-family-professional balance, working for a media company fully run and operated by women. We are a small team of six women, all mothers and all working remote in an incredibly supportive environment that allows me to *have it all*.

NOTES

1. U.S. Citizenship and Immigration Services (2016). *Immigration Reform and Control Act of 1986 (IRCA)*. Washington, DC. Retrieved from https://www.uscis.gov/tools/glossary/immigration-reform-and-control-act-1986-irca

2. Zinn, H. (1980). *A people's history of the United States* (1st ed.). New York, NY.: HarperCollins.

3. 9/11 Memorial and Museum (2018). *FAQ about 9/11*. New York, NY. Retrieved from https://www.911memorial.org/faq-about-911

Chapter Eight

Reconciling Personal and Professional Goals

Fawn-Amber Montoya

"No other success can compensate for failure in the home."[1] I remember this quote cross-stitched, stenciled, and recited in homes throughout my childhood. It was spoken from the pulpit at church, taught in gender-segregated church classes, reiterated on gender-specific Wednesday night activities and often reinforced at home. The greatest success a woman could ever achieve was to be a mother. This narrative still echoes through my mind even 10 years after I stopped attending the Mormon Church. Raised within the religion and in a home that had clearly defined gender roles for my parents, I was lucky to be raised alongside four brothers who did not fully embrace these sexist ideas. The number of boys in the family made it difficult to segregate household chores by gender, and I spent much of my childhood sharing private and public spaces with a cadre of boys. My relationship with my brothers, and their equal treatment of us girls, allowed me to feel comfortable questioning the "roles of women" that had been adhered to so strongly by the women around me.

FAMILIAL AND RELIGIOUS CONSTRUCTIONS OF GENDER

As a young girl, I did not mull over or question the gendered segregation of my religion or of my parents' relationship; it seemed that all I ever I wanted was a similar lifestyle. I felt it at the core of my being, I wanted to serve God, knowing that procreation was ordained of God. Motherhood was going to be my future and there was no need to think otherwise. I even remember crying myself to sleep at eight years old worried that I might never have children, and, if I did, I hoped and prayed that I would be a good mother. It would take years for me to realize how deep this idea of motherhood and segregated gender roles had penetrated into my psyche, and I am still coming to understand the numerous ways that my life choices have been affected because of these ideas that I constructed in my youth.

It is no surprise that these ideas about gender became deeply embedded. When young girls of my religious affiliation were asked what they wanted to be when they grew up, a *mother* was the appropriate response. I bought in to this idea, so whenever I was asked what I wanted to be from the ages of eight to 20 I said I wanted to be a mom. I was also taught in my home and at church to be self-sufficient. Cooking, cleaning, quilting, knitting and canning were common interests during my childhood, and my mother along with other women in my faith community regularly engaged in and encouraged the young girls to participate in these activities. I was being trained and was learning how to be the ideal mother and mate. While I worried about when I would find "The One," I could spend my time working on my motherhood preparations.

As a teenager, my church had a program for young women to develop their talents. Much of the program was based on religious study, self-development, and homemaking skills, and we were assigned leadership positions, named callings, based on our age group. We were told by our leaders that these callings were spiritually inspired; however, what I failed to realize at the time was that most of the outcome of this program was based on who actually showed up and consistently participated. We had opportunities to engage with our female organizers and these occasions resulted in training for leadership. We were also expected to prepare and deliver well thought-out speeches in front of the congregation, which was a daunting task for any young person, but gave me the chance to develop my public speaking skills. And, because of my desire to be devoted, I embraced these opportunities. I wanted to be humble and I was taught that the best path to finding a desirable mate was to behave appropriately so God would provide. Since I wanted a happy marriage and children, I believed that the decisions I made in my youth would have a positive impact on me for the rest of my life.

At first glance, it would be easy to say that my religious upbringing framed my views of motherhood, but there are undercurrents of my Latina identity that also framed my ideas of home life, which I encountered as a child and still continue to impact me today. I grew up mostly in Colorado in a Hispanic household that acknowledged our indigenous roots, but we never explored more than an occasional Pow Wow in New Mexico, an annual hunting trip, and eating of fry bread or beans at home. Growing up, it was not abnormal as a family to discuss the fact that we were Spanish-American, Hispanic, and Native American. Our family heritage was grounded to the southwestern United States, and pinto beans and homemade tortillas were regular meals in our home, but maybe that was more because of our class status than because of our ethnicity.

As most traditional Hispanic families are structured, my father was clearly the head of the household and my mother was responsible for the keeping of the house and raising children. They subscribed to these ideas because each of their parents' marriages actually had blurred gender lines, which they saw as one of the reasons for their parents' unhappiness. Rather than seeing a need to have an egalitarian marriage and open communication, they fell back on the religiously and socially defined gender roles of their generation as an attempt to have a balanced and happy relationship. While this may have been a good management situation for my father, my mother had always had a rebellious streak. She was obedient in public, but questioned his perceived authority to her children. My parents did not segregate their children's chores and activities based on their gender mainly because, I think, there were too many children to keep track of. Also, their parenting styles created unsupervised spaces where my siblings and I openly questioned our parents' dysfunctional marriage and the power of the patriarchy. We could clearly see that following traditional roles was not working as a recipe for marital bliss in our home. However, there were family rules placed on us as children, with the expectation that when we grew up, our primary goal should be to marry someone of our same religious upbringing. And, while my parents encouraged us to go to college, they did not provide any financial or emotional support to help us make it through, believing that "The Lord would provide."

I followed many of my parents' ideas about religion and felt guided in my young life. I embraced leadership opportunities within the church organization throughout my life, and much of what I learned in my younger years still holds true today. I learned that if I showed up and did my job well, then I would be rewarded. The reward, however, was not always how *I wanted* it to be, but my religion embraced the idea that God knew what was best for me, so He would provide me with what I *needed*. The church is structured with informal, lay leadership that gave me the space to envision women in leadership positions at the same time that I saw women as mothers. Therefore, I personally did not see leadership and motherhood working in conflict, although leadership in my faith focused on service and volunteering, and was never about having a career outside the home.

When I graduated from high school, I was headed to a Mormon junior college with the goal of finding a spouse in mind. I had been raised with this idea, and I felt that it was central to my religious identity as a woman. I had also been taught that one of the main goals of marriage was to create an eternal family, which would last beyond death. So, going away to college, and specifically a Mormon college, brought young single Mormons into proximity with each other, creating an environment in which individuals of the same religious ideologies could socialize and build relationships. These spaces, because they were private institutions, could combine religious doctrine with academic research. So, for me, in my late teens and early 20s, the concepts of motherhood and marriage were not just encouraged by my parents, roommates, and religious leaders; they also came into the academic classroom permeating my entire world view.

LEARNING HARD TRUTHS:
A CAREER WOMAN IN THE MAKING

Instead of immediately finding a husband, *The One,* what I found when I began attending college was that I had a brain for complex thinking. It quickly dawned on me that I was either smarter or a harder worker than the rest of the students in my courses, including the disproportionate number of males in the classes that I was enrolled in. I still had my dreams of motherhood, but I quickly realized that raising my hand in class and being a good study partner did not equate to being dateable. Many of my male classmates wanted to date women who followed the gender constructs of our religious culture with marriage as the ultimate goal, and sought to build a household where the husband was the patriarch and the woman was his help mate at home. While it would have been easy to choose as an 18-year-old which of these routes was better to pursue—marriage—I leaned more toward career success because, while I respected a patriarchal structure, I started realizing that it was stifling. At that time, I had neither come to grips with how much of a feminist I was, nor did I understand that my kind of feminism had no space within my faith community. I would spend the next 12 years trying to reconcile what I had been taught in my youth, conflicting with what I had been empowered by in early adulthood. I started to challenge my constructed gender norm and began to rethink my ideas about what I personally wanted to accomplish in life.

Yet, despite my eyes and mind being opened, the social pressure to marry remained present. As I embraced my intellect and began to reframe my long-term professional goals, my parents, peers and friends felt conflicted for me. During my sophomore year of college, I lived with four other women of whom I was not acquainted with before moving in. I lived in a college town, and, out of the four women, only one of them was enrolled full time at the university. She had a fiancé, which culturally meant that she escaped the constant onslaught of social critique encouraging marriage. My roommates who were not enrolled at the university had come to Utah both for the social experience of being in a space where other adults embraced Mormonism, and also because their home communities had few eligible Mormon bachelors. These girls believed that being roommates meant that we should try to be good friends and they sought out opportunities for us to spend social time together.

What they quickly found was that I took my education very seriously. I would leave every morning before 8 a.m. and spend my day on campus, not usually returning home before 9 p.m. I typically took a 15-18-credit-hour course load, worked on campus on a part-time basis, and spent a good amount of time studying at the library. On the weekends, I studied some more with my brother, as he and I were both Pell Grant and merit-scholarship recipients, and needed to maintain our strong academic standing. Within a month of living with my roommates, they had come to the conclusion that I must be a "man-hating" career woman. I was simply a 19-year-old college student, focusing on my studies, which was enough for them to brand me as an infidel. I vividly remember one morning as I was getting ready for my busy day that one of my roommates came into my bathroom telling me that she and two other roommates were concerned about me. They worried that I was going to *burn out*. They did not want me to have a breakdown because I was working *too hard,* and they felt that, as a woman, I needed more balance in my life.

Their solution to my career-woman problem was for me to either get married or to prepare myself to go on an 18-month proselyting mission for the church. They decided the best way to *fix me,* though, was to force me to date. One weekend soon after the school year had started, they set me up on a blind date with another resident of our apartment complex. They decided that this would be a group date to make it more difficult for me to try to get out of it. When Friday night came, they stood in the kitchen telling me that I had to go and how rude it would be of me if I did not, so I gave in. This would be one of many awkward social situations during my college years that made me wonder if the social constrictions of gender with which I had grown up were ideals that I could indeed continue to adhere to.

While there were social situations within my religion that made me question my ability to reconcile motherhood and my profession, my romantic relationships throughout my educational experience were also called into question. Much of this situation was based on my new-found internal conflict with the patriarchal system enforced by the members of my church. During my senior year of college, I was casually dating a man who was about to graduate from college, and we went out to dinner with another couple that had recently become engaged. I had learned to keep my professional aspirations out of many conversations, but this conversation turned to the subject of the female partner's decision to change her last name after marriage. I mentioned that I had no plans to do this and that I felt that keeping my maiden name post marriage would be important in my future professional endeavors. My date's quick response was "Well, you won't be marrying me!" In that moment, and still today, I wonder how the idea of keeping one's maiden name made someone an impossible marriage prospect.

Years later, while in graduate school, I continued to date within my religious culture mainly because I did not feel comfortable leaving my faith community, and also because I felt socially out of place in non-religious social spaces. I was also worried that my family would not accept me for whom I married if he did not share the same faith background as mine. I wanted to find someone who they would approve of, but also someone who would respect my religious worldviews.

I developed friendships with other women in graduate school, but I did not seek out relationships with men outside of the Mormon realm. Some of this behavior was driven by fear, since I had been taught that "you marry who you date," and also that marrying out of the faith meant damning my children to an uncertain future. I knew that whether I embraced it or not, I could survive the patriarchal structure, and I was not yet comfortable walking away from my social connections within Mormonism. The majority of my immediate and extended family had married within the faith and I was concerned that I would be ostracized for not following this model.

In seeking this ideal future that would please both myself and my family, motherhood and career had to be synonymous for me during my professional preparation in my 20s. I believed that by focusing on my education and professional development I would be able to find a career that would be flexible enough to allow me to raise children. I did not anticipate that I would work less than full time, but I planned for a career that I could work at least a quarter of the time from home, even if it meant working nights and weekends, while still making a salary. Socially, within my religious culture and in my dating life, this idea did not translate. Either, I did not feel the need to spell it out to the men I dated, or I had reached the point where I knew that, as soon as I mentioned a career, I would already be labeling myself as *undateable*. Even though I was completing my graduate work in a non-religious environment, I felt the pressure to marry.

On the other hand, I also loved to learn. I thrived on opening a new book. Writing was second nature, academic dialogue thrilled my whole being, and I loved the feeling of making connections between my textbooks and my classes. I craved the stimulation, and I realized that in this space I could follow a path for me to be able to have a career in the academy, which would give me enough flexibility to build a family. At that age, I was optimistic and believed that I would one day encounter a Mormon man who would agree to being married to a feminist Mormon academic. They are out there, I just did not find one, nor did I marry one of them.

I had relationships where men asked me to consider changing graduate programs or dropping out of school all together to align with *their* career and professional goals. At one point in a relationship, Paul, who I dated off and on in my 20s, mentioned that if I spent as much time on our relationship as I did in school, that we would already have been married. He was very clear that he felt that my career aspirations should be second to the goal of raising a family. I believe that I had never put these in competition with each other, however, this was not how he—and most other men of my faith—had interpreted my drive and ambition.

Years later, in 2016, Paul contacted me. We had not communicated for over 10 years, but we had seen each other's profiles on social media. By this time, I was already married, and had two biological children while he still had none, and he mentioned to me that he had never thought that I was going to have children. I thought about what he said for a while, and I realized that he had formed these expectations of me years earlier because I was so career-focused that children could not possibly, in his views, be in my future. I racked my brain thinking about at what point in our relationship I had said that I did not want children. I do not recall ever mentioning this, but he had somehow equated a career focus as not wanting a family at all. Therefore, he had chosen a wife expecting that she would be a stay-at-home mom raising four or five children rather than someone whom he thought had chosen a career over children. He lamented his frustration to me not only with not having any children yet, but with the financial limitations that he faced with his wife having no education and no motivation to find suitable employment.

RELIGIOUS SPACES FOR LEADERSHIP

Going back to my graduate school years, despite the social awkwardness, I remained an active Mormon during that phase of my life. The church had student congregations housed near universities, which allowed members of the similar ages to worship and fraternize with each other, creating an environment that allowed for social interactions which would hopefully culminate in marriage. From 2002-05, I served as the local president of the Relief Society, the women's organization within the church. In this position, I attended weekly meetings with older male (55-70 years of age), in which we discussed the structure of the local organization and how to best help congregants. These older men ran the meetings, supervising the one women's organization as well as the men's organizations. All leadership roles were assigned to men, except for my position, in which I had two female assistants.

Through this service opportunity, I developed professional management skills from these weekly meetings as well as quarterly trainings with the regional level of our congregation. Because of the religious nature of this position, though, I have never put it on a résumé. And, looking back, I feel that this role reinforced the patriarchal culture of the church because, in some ways, I find that while these trainings did make me equal to my male counterparts, I was not always privy to other congregational matters, which were saved for priesthood-only (men) meetings. In 2013, the Ordain Women organization, a group of men and women within the Mormon church even raised the issue of whether or not the church should confer the priesthood authority to women, breaking gender barriers in positions of authority in the organization. This issue stemmed from the fact that the church was founded on the idea that the highest levels of leadership and access to spiritual guidance are directly linked to biblical ideas of leadership from the Old Testament in the *Bible*, with the passing on of this gift from God as being intended only for men. Therefore, within Mormonism, the highest positions of leadership are only open to men.[2]

However, despite my mere contributions as a woman in the congregation, the expertise I acquired in this leadership service has not only helped me to manage my household, but they were also a source of excellent training for my career today as I find myself still sitting alongside several older men in meetings with university administration. In 2005, I decided to step down from my position in the church, when I was told that the man in charge of all of the local congregations in the region felt that I was not encouraging marriage and motherhood to the young adult women under my leadership. This left me feeling frustrated. When I had accepted the position, the four women who had served before me had all been honorably released from their callings because they had gotten married within two years of serving. The congregation even joked that the only way to leave the Relief Society presidency position in our local community was to get married. So, after the criticism from the regional leader, I decided to step away from this position and focus solely on completing my dissertation for my doctoral degree.

That same year, I accepted a doctoral fellowship at Texas Tech University. This appointment resulted in me moving from my home of six years, and leaving behind "potential marriage partners." By the time I accepted this academic position, I had reconciled that my professional career needed to be my primary focus. I had tried to maintain a dating life, but the demands of graduate school made such efforts increasingly difficult. For me, my religion was based on Christianity and not on defining myself as a mother. The older I became, the more I embraced this idea rather than my childhood belief in obedience for the long-term pay off of marriage. I had been in Arizona for over seven years and had come to the conclusion that my dating life had stagnated. There were three men with whom I had strong friendships and casual dating interactions, but none of them had become serious about long-term relationships. At no point in my years in graduate school did I ever decide that I did not *want* a relationship, marriage or children. The Mormon cultural influences in my life created this artificial illusion of incompatibility between a professional future and the establishment of family for the men I dated. I was always a good *friend*, but I was never considered *the marrying type*. I stayed faithful to the church during this time, and I also had opportunities for leadership both as a teacher and as a volunteer at the local Mormon temple in Texas. These opportunities not only honed my organizational skills, but also allowed me to continue to face the reality that I had come to accept: Motherhood did not appear to be in my near future as long as I focused on my career.

When I moved to Lubbock, I attended a new congregation of my church. The standard was that individuals under the age of 30 were allowed to attend student worship meetings, but once one turned 30, he or she needed to consider attending the family meetings. I was lucky because I had not yet reached my "expiration date," but I was five years older than the *dateable* women in my congregation, and I was three years more advanced in my graduate program than the other women my age. The *dateable* women were usually recent high school graduates or younger students starting their university career. This meant that they had not yet begun to envision themselves as having a career, so they came across as non-threatening to men. They did not read the newspaper daily or watch the news, which made them more malleable in the long run. They were more concerned with having a good time than with being critically engaged in the world around them.

Since I did not necessarily fit the profile my male peers had set for a future wife, I had learned early on in my academic career not to share too much information about my long-term plans of having a professional career with fellow congregants because I did not want the unsolicited commentary or advice. I was tired of the comments and suggestions about what I should do to make myself more physically attractive, how I should do my hair, wear my makeup or flirt. I was constantly reminded that men wanted someone who was feminine, smiley, good-natured, and less politically inclined. It felt like there was a constant desire for others to have input regarding what they thought that I should do to please men. I learned in my early 20s that "men of the faith" were not interested in women who did not seek motherhood as their primary focus, and my liberal stance on politics, and keeping my own maiden name had suddenly ended a number of my relationships because these ideas made me not dating material to these men. When I was introduced to other individuals within my religion, they would typically ask:

New Acquaintance: "What are you studying in school?"

Me: "History."

New Acquaintance: "What are you going to do with that?"

Me: "I want to be a professor."

New Acquaintance: "That takes a really long time. . . . You have to get a master's degree and a Ph.D. . . . What about a family?"

It came to the point where I tried my hardest to avoid these conversations, and eventually spent less time in places where I would have to answer for my life's decisions to complete strangers.

I felt more comfortable in the academy and began to limit my relationships with those of my religion. In order to manage the demands of graduate school and of my religion, I had three groups of friends for support: work friends, church friends, and school friends. I had begun working at the athletics department at the University of Arizona as an academic tutor. This allowed me to work at nights and to socially engage with other women who were also unmarried and working on their doctorates. This space made me realize that being unmarried in my 20s was actually not abnormal. At the same time, I still had a small social circle of people who shared my religious background and, together, we attended sporting events, exercised and watched movies. There were two years before we all headed off to complete our graduate careers or begin full-time jobs where we did not feel confined by our faith's social world. Then, there were also my school friends. There were some people who identified as lesbians, queer, trans, and also other feminists like me. These friends were the ones who allowed me to feel comfortable attending my first drag show and allowed me the space to see the conflicts between what I wanted and what I had been taught. We were all just trying to survive the rigors of the academy, while learning about who we truly were.

THE WORKING MOTHER

It has now been 10 years since I was an active Mormon and also 10 years since I married my Catholic husband. I still see my former work and graduate school friends at least every two years. In regards to my church friends, I see their posts on social media and there have been occasional visits if I make time in between visiting my other friends. Two years ago, I decided to travel with my children to Arizona to visit my old work and school friends, and I decided to stop at the home of my church friends who had happened to marry each other. The wife, Emily, a stay-at-home mother with seven children, joked that she and her husband Nathan were glad that I decided to have a few *token children.* They said, "It helps that you had one boy and one girl, then you don't have to try for a third. That would really mess up your career." Stop! Just stop! For years, I had been criticized for not having children and now I was being critiqued for not having *enough* of them. In this moment, I was mostly sad that my relationships had not stood the test of time because I had not stayed active within the Mormon church, and now we had nothing in common.

I no longer tried to fit into the mold of my religious upbringing. However, my problems were not over since the academy can be just as critical of me choosing to have had children as Mormonism was when I did not. It can be just as difficult in a professional setting with many of my peers choosing to not have children and others beginning their professional academic career when their children are grown. I have also found that there are very few women of color in the academy and those with young children are even fewer. So, when I became pregnant with my first child, I had to navigate the political implications of this decision in the workplace.

When I first had my son, my department chair mentioned that there would be no problem with him coming to meetings with me or being on campus, but what I quickly found was this was not the case. I brought him to one department meeting when he was six months old, and he tried to crawl across the table. At three months old, I had brought him to class; I stood at the front of the class, introduced the film and sat down. The two-minute moment of my son being in front of the class resulted in a student writing a course evaluation that said that I should not have taken my baby to school. In typical double standard fashion, I have male colleagues who bring their children to campus, the children are disruptive in meetings and go to class for 50 minutes, but these men are seen as good fathers, and their children were *cute,* while I felt that I was being judged harshly for mine being unruly. I had vowed when I first had my children that I would not hide my motherhood from my professional career, however, a professional career is not always open to mothering young children.

I still dread those days when my children are sick and I have to take them to campus with me, or the occasional last-minute meeting when I bring my four-year-old, who chooses to climb up the wall. I have been lucky to be saved by younger peers who are juggling motherhood as well, or who are assisting their siblings with child rearing. I have taken my oldest child to professional conferences, but only those based on Women's Studies or on Hispanic Studies because these spaces are more open to the combination of motherhood and a career, and I feel like my Latina identity can be genuine to my role as a mother. I still cringe when my child makes a move in the back of the room or when he meets award-winning scholars and is not impressed by them. I am grateful for the conferences that provide childcare, but saddened when my peers head out late at night for a drink, and I am stuck in the hotel room spending time with my child. I am learning to accept that my relationship with my children is valuable and that the times when we travel will pay off later. I feel as if I have betrayed my gender, my ethnicity, and any religious teachings when I crave to just have one night out with colleagues away from children.

FIND A MENTOR

I experience frustration with my non-academic colleagues when they tell me that their children have to adjust to their life, and that they teach their children that "Mom comes before children" and that "Children need to just get on board and adjust." Most of these women are not Latinas. My mentor from graduate school is the one woman whom I trust most when it comes to the balance between her career and her mothering. She is respected in her profession, but over the past 20 years I have seen her as she has put her daughter first in her life. She still presents at conferences and has worked in administration at large universities. She understands the importance of my career to me, and has seen how hard I have worked to get into my academic position, but she also understands that children need to be a priority.

One example of the need for a mentor who understands the difficulties with having a career and being a mother occurred in 2013. I was appointed to the Ludlow Massacre Centennial Commission by the governor of the State of Colorado. The ceremony would occur in his office at the state capital, and the appointment was to be made on April 2. My youngest child was born on March 29, so I was conflicted. My daughter's due date was supposed to have been April 19, and I had expected her to be on time because her sibling was. As soon as I went into labor I started to panic. I did not know how I would be able to manage the two-hour drive to and from Denver and the other one hour of waiting for the governor with a four-day old child. Should I bring her with me? Do I leave her at home? Do I take her to Denver, but leave her with family? I do not believe that a newborn child should be in a car seat for more than the 30 minutes it may take to drive them to or from a hospital or doctor's office.

When I spoke about my predicament to my female colleagues who have children of their own children, they told me that my daughter would be fine with someone else watching her, and that a bottle of formula would get my child through the five hours without me. I was torn. I was physically able to make the trip, but I knew that I would worry about my daughter the entire time. I was also a firm believer in breastfeeding and I knew that the first few weeks were essential to establishing a milk supply. That Sunday, I called my mentor because, in that moment, I knew that she was the only person who would understand my perspective since she had known me from the time I was 22, had read much of my work, and her own research had been the foundation for my work. Her simple response, understanding that being appointed to a state commission commemorating a 100-year event was an once-in-a-lifetime experience, was to stay home and take care of my daughter. She said that it was an important professional moment, but I would regret more not caring for my daughter in those early weeks. I made the phone call on Monday to the governor's office to regretfully inform them that I would not be able to attend. Providentially, they had moved the commission appointments to April 19. Through this experience, I learned that when it came to being a mother and having a career it is important to find other women who have experience in balancing these two worlds, whose opinion you trust and who understand your perspective.

LATINAS AND CHILDREN

"Latinas in their early 30s with no children do not exist," was the response from my husband's family when we first started dating. In my early 30s, I had finally figured out that I did not belong with my religious peers and that I could manage to be happy without them. I had secured a tenure-track position at a regional comprehensive university and recently moved from Lubbock, Texas back to Colorado. I had accepted that I was ready to have children, and I had met a man who wanted to marry me despite my feminist ways. He did not need me to take his last name, he did not think that one's religion should govern their life choices, and he was willing to relocate for my career.

Here I sat in the kitchen of my future in-laws, explaining that I did not have any children because I had *chosen* not to have children thus far. I felt like I had swapped my being out of place in my religious community with feeling out of place in my ethnicity and my gender groups. How could I have possibly chosen not to have children? I also lived alone! They would have had fewer concerns about me if I would have had three children from three different men than they did about the fact that I had chosen to not have children and to live on my own. "What had you been doing all this time?" is the question that still confounds my husband's family. A typical conversation exchange among them would go as this:

Brother-in-law: "What does she do?"

My husband: "She writes and teaches."

Brother-in-law: "Like books?"

My husband: "Yes."

Brother-in-law: "What does she write about and teach?"

My husband: "She writes and teaches about being Latina in the United States."

There is always a questioning look followed with an "I see…" look.

After 10 years of marriage, his family still does not know what I do for work, and I continue to meet more family members who ask the same questions. I teach Mexican-American History and Culture and I treat my students like *familia*. When my White male colleagues wonder why I am so beloved by students, I tell them it is because I am Latina; I listen to *Intocable,* I eat beans and tortillas, and I speak enough Spanish to get by. At the Hispanic-serving institution where I work, the professoriate is predominately White, so being a Latina with a Ph.D. has opened up amazing possibilities.

While I had concerns about having a harmonious relationship between being a good mother and having a career, both of these parts of my life occurred at a parallel time. I began my tenure-track position in August of 2007, and soon after I got married in December of that same year. I had my second child in March of 2013, and I was granted tenure and promotion just a month later, in April. I have chosen a career in which I have been able to be successful at a university, but that also allows me to fulfill my childhood goals of marriage and motherhood.

However, my vision of motherhood has changed over the past 20 years, as well as my religious and spiritual perspectives. Much of this transformation is embodied within the form of a major Catholic religious icon, La Virgen de Guadalupe. La Virgen De Guadalupe appeared to an indigenous convert, Juan Diego, and therefore to the Catholic church. Her appearance on a hill in Tepeyac in Mexico City in the 1500s is considered a miracle by the Catholic church, which makes her the patroness of the Americas, and she is worshipped by many as a Brown-skinned version of the Virgin Mary. For me, I turn to La Virgen de Guadalupe to frame my spiritual beliefs not because of her connections to Catholicism, but because of her roots in Aztec tradition as Tonantzin, the fertility goddess who the Spanish recreated into the Brown-skinned patroness of the Americas.[3] I think about her in this space caught between two worlds, and I found that Latinos(as) were willing to embrace her. So, I felt that if I embraced her, my religion, ethnicity, gender, and motherhood were not to be questioned anymore. I felt like I could embrace her as Tonantzin and Mother Earth, and Latinos would not think too much about what I really thought of her because they just assume I am being a good Catholic.

The fruits of my years of sacrifice and determination to develop my career has led to the reality that I have had a faster increase in my salary than my partner has. While we started off in a similar economic situation, over the past 10 years, I have clearly become the bread winner with his income being supplemental to mine. The difficulty has never been with how much money I make, but with the hours that I work. While we have a similar workload, mine is staggered throughout the day with me being responsible for child drop off and pick up because of his long shifts. I have to share my work time with my parenting duties. I often find myself writing, emailing, and prepping for classes at my kitchen table between 10 p.m. and 2 a.m. My husband's workload, on the other hand, stays within a 6 a.m. to 4 p.m. block. I do not know if he has figured out yet how much I can accomplish between the late-night hours, and still have the energy to drag my body out of bed and have my kids ready for school on time the next day.

I also chose to marry a Latino, which was a conscious choice because I feel that I am constantly faced with the idea that I might not be Latina enough. I was born in the United States with roots in the southwestern United States that predate the Spanish conquest. I grew up in a family in which there were debates surrounding our ethnicity, including my extended family arguing at every gathering whether we are Hispanic, Native American, Spanish-American or Mexican-American, but I decided a long time ago to not engage in these discussions because it has been the same debate for 40 years. I believe that my classroom is my space for debate and discussion about ethnic identity, not my home. I have also decided to not share too much about my work life with my relatives, either. This probably started when I chose to limit my conversations about my career progress in the church setting back in graduate school. However, I have also found that family space is more acceptable to discuss children rather than discussing a recent professional appearance on C-SPAN or PBS, or the award that you receive at your university. Family members rarely allow you to forget your childhood follies, and they find ways of critiquing you over time spent raising children or asking about your spiritual beliefs. These are questions that I have chosen to avoid discussing publicly because I do not think that random and persistent comments from extended family members, such as "Family time is prime time," should be responded to. I also do not think that I need to rationalize my life choices to anyone.

MOTHERHOOD IN ACADEMIA

Today, as my children grow and I find myself entering a mid-career phase, I still make personal and professional decisions around what I perceive as being best for my them. I have accepted that this is based more on my upbringing than on my personal desires. While I do not see our happiness intertwined, I have a desire to be a good parent not because of what people think about me, but because I want to have friends when I am older. I want my children to be able to come to me about personal and professional advice, but I have also discovered that they are my companions on this journey through life.

In order to maintain both my professional work and my household, I have found that I need to create clear dividing lines. I hide my profession from my home and I hide my children from my profession. I continue to hear those voices from my youth about the need for me to be in the home. I make sacrifices for my children when it comes to my profession, and I sacrifice some professional gains for the good of the family. To me, this does not feel hollow, superficial or constructed. I enjoy being a parent, not because I was taught to do this or because I was expected to; I choose this life because it makes me happy and fulfilled. I do not think that my children are any different than they would have been if I would have chosen motherhood only over a career, or if I would have had them earlier in life. There was no rush to be a mother; that came in its own time and my decision to free myself from religious doctrine would have probably also happened even if I had become a mother at a younger age.

What I do find to be true is that I continue to shroud my motherhood status from my professional positions. This does not mean that I hide my desire for children, but sometimes the joy that I get from being with them. There are some meetings that I choose not to go to simply for the fact that I would rather be at home with my son and daughter. When there are community events, I do not attend some of them because I would rather be with my children. For me, motherhood has become a space to be able to separate myself from the professional realm. My parenting—not just motherhood because I do not believe that my parenting is gender-based—is about establishing a structure. I have established my own boundaries and a space to rest from professional pressures. When I am home, I limit my internet and phone usage, and the weekends are about my children and not about work. I cannot say I enjoy the labor involved in parenting or the time that it takes, but I do like being able to use my parenting to assist me in achieving a home-life balance.

Today, I do not think of myself as a *career woman*. I see myself, as I imagine other women do, as someone who has chosen a profession that I love and in which I can excel, and someone who has chosen to have a family that I put first because then I am able to set boundaries in my professional world.

NOTES

1. McKay, D. O. (1964). First day morning meeting. *One Hundred Thirty-Fourth Annual Conference of The Church of Jesus Christ of Latter-day Saints.* 5. Retrieved from https://archive.org/stream/conferencereport1964a#page/n5/mode/2up/search/success

2. Evans, W. & Mikita, C. (2013, October 5). Debate over LDS women's roles spotlighted in protest. *KSL Broadcasting.* Retrieved from https://www.ksl.com/?sid=27133883

3. Carrillo, W. (2010, December 13). El dia de la Virgen de Guadalupe: A reflection. *Huffington Post.* Retrieved from https://www.huffingtonpost.com/wendy-carrillo/la-virgen-marias-birthday_b_795435.html

Conclusion

The heartfelt stories shared by the Latinas in this book illustrate the undeniable prevalence of gender, age, ethnicity and cultural biases in leadership still present to this day. Some accounts emphasized gender, others examined the complexities of the authors' specific cultural demands, while others incorporated several of the biases above. Every chapter, though, provided optimistic solutions and a vision for individual growth, transforming evidently unfavorable personal and professional experiences into encouragement for positive outcomes at home and the workplace.

Through these narratives, it also became clear that a great deal of people with whom we come in contact are not prepared to respond to situations that are unfamiliar to them. Some of these people might behave in such a way, even maliciously, due to prejudice that has been ingrained in them for one reason or another. Others, in contrast, have simply not been previously exposed to much gender, age, ethnicity and other types of cultural diversity. Therefore, regardless of the reason why these negative interactions occur, when trying to silence biases in leadership, all parties should be willing to attempt to understand one another, adjust themselves when facing new situations, and seek to develop their cultural intelligence capacity.

Cultural intelligence denotes a person's ability to operate, to connect with others, and to make decisions effectively in multiple cultural environments. This translates to employees with higher levels of cultural intelligence thriving across the globe because they can adapt more easily.[1] However, cultural intelligence is *not* an all-or-nothing capacity; it is a flexible aptitude, which can be strengthened through education, observation and intercultural contact.[2, 3] With this in mind, learning tools, such as the present book, are made available with the intent of assisting leaders, workers, students, and people in all roles in society to gain more knowledge about cultures and subcultures different from their own. In turn, this increased understanding, can help silence an array of biases and improve one's cultural intelligence and his or her ability to work with others from dissimilar backgrounds.

And since leaders aim for success in their position of authority, it becomes important to remember, once again, that cultural intelligence is key to eliminating biases in positions of leadership, and attaining positive interpersonal results.[4] It is my hope that, soon, all Latinas and other minorities will learn to silence the negative interactions based on gender, age, ethnicity and cultural biases that they encounter. The days when we minorities are told that we should not—or *cannot*—pursue professional success and personal achievements must come to an end. It is up to us to turn around and educate others, telling the world that, yes, of course, we can do it!

NOTES

1. Kim, Y., & Van Dyne, L. (2012). Cultural intelligence and international leadership potential: The importance of contact for members of the majority. *Applied Psychology: An International Review, 61*(2), 272–294. doi:10.1111/j.1464-0597.2011.00468.x

2. Earley, P.C., & Ang, S. (2003). *Cultural intelligence: Individual interactions across cultures.* Palo Alto, CA: Stanford University Press.

3. Kim, Y., & Van Dyne, L. (2012). Cultural intelligence and international leadership potential: The importance of contact for members of the majority. *Applied Psychology: An International Review, 61*(2), 272-294. doi:10.1111/j.1464-0597.2011.00468.x

4. Avolio, J., Walumbwa, F. O., & Weber, T. J. (2009). Leadership: Current theories, research, and future directions. *Annual Review of Psychology, 60*, 421–449. doi:10.1146/annurev.psych.60.110707.163621

References

9/11 Memorial and Museum (2018). *FAQ about 9/11*. New York, NY. Retrieved from https://www.911memorial.org/faq-about-911

Amnesty International (n.d.). *The Ginetta Sagan award*. Retrieved from https://www.amnestyusa.org/about-us/grants-and-awards/ginetta-sagan-award/

Avolio, J., Walumbwa, F. O., & Weber, T. J. (2009). Leadership: Current theories, research, and future directions. *Annual Review of Psychology, 60*, 421–449. doi:10.1146/annurev.psych.60.110707.163621

Bennis, W. G., & Thomas, R. J. (2010). Crucibles of leadership. In J. T. McMahon (Ed.), *Leadership classics* (pp. 559–568). Long Grove, IL: Waveland Press, Inc.

Carrillo, W. (2010, December 13). El dia de la Virgen de Guadalupe: A reflection. *Huffington Post*. Retrieved from https://www.huffingtonpost.com/wendy-carrillo/la-virgen-marias-birthday_b_795435.html

Combs, S. (2008). *Texas in focus*. Austin, Tex.: Texas Comptroller of Public Accounts, Research and Analysis Division. Retrieved from http://www.window.state.tx.us/specialrpt/tif/southtexas/pdf/SouthTexasFullReport.pdf

Covey, S. R. (2004). *The 8th habit: From effectiveness to greatness*. New York, NY: Free Press.

Cox, C. B. (2010). *The role of age in causal attributions for poor performance: Target and rater effects*. Retrieved from ProQuest Digital Dissertations. (AAT 3421436)

Earley, P.C., & Ang, S. (2003). *Cultural intelligence: Individual interactions across cultures*. Palo Alto, CA: Stanford University Press.

Eccles, J. S. (1989). Bringing young women to math and science. In M. Crawford & M. Gentry (Eds.), *Gender and thought: Psychological Perspectives* (pp. 33–58). New York: Springer-Verlag.

Equal Employment Opportunity Commission (n.d.). *Age discrimination*. Washington, DC. Retrieved from https://www.eeoc.gov/laws/types/age.cfm.

Ersoy, N., Born, M., Derous, E., & Molen, H. T. (2012). The effect of cultural orientation and leadership style on self- versus other-oriented organizational citizenship behaviour in Turkey and the Netherlands. *Asian Journal of Social Psychology, 15*(4), 249–260. doi:10.1111/j.1467-839X.2012.01380.x

Evans, W. & Mikita, C. (2013, October 5). Debate over LDS women's roles spotlighted in protest. *KSL Broadcasting*. Retrieved from https://www.ksl.com/?sid=27133883

Drucker, P. F. (2010). Managing oneself. In J. T. McMahon (Ed.), *Leadership classics* (pp. 524–536). Long Grove, IL: Waveland Press, Inc.

Fung, W. C. (2015). An interdependent view on women in leadership. *Asia Journal of Theology, 29*(1), 117–138.

Gardner, J. W. (1990). *On leadership.* New York, N.Y.: The Free Press.

George, B. (2003). *Authentic leadership: Rediscovering the secrets to creating lasting value.* San Francisco, Calif.: Jossey-Bass.

George, B., & Sims, P. (2007). *True North: Discover your authentic leadership.* San Francisco, Calif.: Jossey-Bass.

Hansson, P. H., & Andersen, J. A. (2007). The Swedish principal: Leadership style, decision-making style, and motivation profile. *International Journal of Leadership in Learning, 11*(8), 1–13.

Heider, J. (1986). The Tao of leadership: Lao Tzu's Tao Te Ching adapted for a new age . Atlanta, Ga.: Humanics New Age.

Herbst, T. H., & Conradie, P. P. (2011). Leadership effectiveness in higher education: Managerial self-perceptions versus perceptions of others. *SAJIP: South African Journal of Industrial Psychology, 37*(1), 1–14. doi:10.4102/sajip.v37i1.867

Hofstede, G. (1980). *Culture's consequences: International differences in work-related values.* Beverly Hills, Calif.: Sage Publications.

Hofstede, G. (2001). *Culture's consequences: comparing values, behaviors, institutions and organizations across nations* (2nd ed.). Thousand Oaks, Calif.: Sage.

Hofstede, G. (2006). What did GLOBE really measure? Researchers' minds versus respondents' minds. *Journal of International Business Studies, 37*(6), 882–896. doi:http://dx.doi.org/10.1057/palgrave.jibs.8400233

Hofstede, G. H., Hofstede, G. J., & Minkov, M. (2010). *Cultures and organizations: Software of the mind: Intercultural cooperation and its importance for survival* (3rd ed.). New York: McGraw-Hill

Holman Bible Publishers (2017). *The Christian Standard Bible,* 1 Corinthians 4:3-6.

Jayakumar, U. M. (2008). Can higher education meet the needs of an increasingly diverse and global society? Campus diversity and cross-cultural workforce competencies. *Harvard Educational Review, 78*(4), 615–651.

Kasumovic, M. M., & Kuznekoff, J. H. (2015). Insights into sexism: Male status and performance moderates female-directed hostile and amicable behaviour. *Plos ONE, 10*(7), 1–14. doi:10.1371/journal.pone.0131613

Kellerman, B. & Rhode, D. (Eds.). (2007). *Women and leadership: The state of play and strategies for change.* San Francisco, CA: Jossey-Bass.

Kim, Y., & Van Dyne, L. (2012). Cultural intelligence and international leadership potential: The importance of contact for members of the majority. *Applied Psychology: An International Review, 61*(2), 272-294. doi:10.1111/j.1464-0597.2011.00468.x

Kumar, R., Anjum, B., and Sinha, A. (2011). Cross-cultural interactions and leadership behaviour. *Researchers World: Journal of Arts, Science and Commerce 2*(3). 151–160.

Lonner, W. J. (2004). JCCP at 35: Commitment, continuity, and creative adaptation. *Journal of Cross-Cultural Psychology 35*(2). 123–136.

Mankowski, E. S., Galvez, G., and Glass, N. (2011). Interdisciplinary linkage of community psychology and cross-cultural psychology: History, values, and an illustrative research and action project on intimate partner violence. *American Journal of Community Psychology 47* (1/2). 127–143.

McKay, D. O. (1964). First day morning meeting. *One Hundred Thirty-Fourth Annual Conference of The Church of Jesus Christ of Latter-day Saints.* 5. Retrieved from https://archive.org/stream/conferencereport1964a#page/n5/mode/2up/search/success

Monson, T. S. (1997). The mighty strength of the relief society. *Ensign.* Retrieved from https://www.lds.org/ensign/1997/11/the-mighty-strength-of-the-relief-society?lang=eng

Montoya, C. A. (2016). Overcoming impediments: The influence of culture and gender as obstacles and catalysts in leadership development. *Journal of Leadership and Management. 1*(7-8), 41–46.

Montoya, C. A., & Montoya, J. (2015). Cultural awareness in leadership strategy and marketing: Applying Hofstede's basic dilemmas to Brazil. *Journal of Leadership and Management. 1*(3), 13–20.

Moraes, A., & Perkins, P. E. (2007). Women, equity and participatory water management in Brazil. *International Feminist Journal of Politics, 9*(4), 485–493. doi:10.1080/14616740701607986

Northouse, P. (2013). *Leadership: Theory and practice* (6th ed.). Thousand Oaks, Calif.: Sage.

Quote Ambition. (2018). *75 Maya Angelou Quotes on love, life, courage, and women*. Retrieved from http://www.quoteambition.com/maya-angelou-quotes-love-life-courage-women/

Radin, J. (2015). Belong. On *Onward and Sideways*. Los Angeles: Glass Bead Music.

Ramundo Staduto, J. A., Alves Nascimento, C., & de Souza, M. (2013). Ocupações e renda das mulheres e homens no rural do estado do Paraná, Brasil: Uma perspectiva de gênero. (Portuguese) [Occupations and earning of women and men in the rural areas in the state of Paraná, Brazil: A gender perspective.]. *Cuadernos De Desarrollo Rural, 10*(72), 91–115.

Shaw, P. (2014). 'New treasures with the old': Addressing culture and gender imperialism in higher level theological education. *Evangelical Review of Theology, 38*(3), 265–279.

Stogdill, R. M. (1948). Personal factors associated with leadership: A survey of the literature. *Journal of Psychology, 25*, 35–71.

Swim, J. K., & Cohen, L. L. (1997). Overt, covert, and subtle sexism: A comparison between the attitudes toward women and modern sexism scales. *Psychology of Women Quarterly, 21*, 103–118. doi:10.1111/j.1471-6402.1997.tb00103.x.

Taylor, C. (1992). *The ethics of authenticity*. Cambridge, MA: Harvard University Press

The Church of Jesus Christ of Latter-day Saints. (1995). *The family: A proclamation to the world*. Retrieved from https://www.lds.org/bc/content/shared/content/english/pdf/language-materials/36035_eng.pdf?lang=eng

The Church of Jesus Christ of Latter-day Saints. (2009). *Young women personal progress*. Retrieved from https://www.lds.org/bc/content/shared/content/english/pdf/language-materials/36035_eng.pdf?lang=eng

Travis, M. A. (2014). Disabling the gender pay gap: Lessons from the social model of disability. *Denver University Law Review, 91*(4), 893–923.

U.S. Census Bureau (2005). *Household Income – Distribution by Income Level and State: 2005*. Washington, DC. Retrieved from http://www.census.gov/compendia/statab/ tables/08s0684.xls.

U.S. Census Bureau (2010). *The Hispanic Population: 2010*. Washington, DC. Retrieved from http://www.census.gov/prod/cen2010/briefs/c2010br-04.pdf

U.S. Census Bureau (2016). *QuickFacts: Brownsville City, Texas*. Retrieved from https://www.census.gov/quickfacts/fact/table/brownsvillecitytexas/INC110216.

U.S. Citizenship and Immigration Services (2016). *Immigration Reform and Control Act of 1986 (IRCA)*. Washington, DC. Retrieved from https://www.uscis.gov/tools/glossary/immigration-reform-and-control-act-1986-irca

Zinn, H. (1980). *A people's history of the United States* (1st ed.). New York, NY.: HarperCollins.

Index

About the Contributors

Veronica Carrera was born in Ecuador, where she was raised until her early adolescence, when she moved to Miami, Florida. With an MBA from Cornell University and a bachelor's in French, Carrera has had a successful career with more than 17 years of experience in financial markets, working with institutional investors and multinational corporations around the world. Additionally, Carrera is an experienced public and motivational speaker. Her platforms and audiences include venture capitalists, The United Nations, The High School of Economics, and The Grace Institute, a domestic violence organization. She is also an avid triathlete, who completed her first Ironman in 2012.

Dr. Julieta V. García was born in Brownsville, Texas, and was named the first female Mexican-American president of a U.S. college or university in 1986. Her presidency spanned 28 years and was marked by her innovation in conceiving and implementing new higher education models in response to a rapidly changing higher education ecosystem. García has devoted her life's work to higher education, focused on sustaining the democracy of our nation by empowering next generation college students. In 2009, *Time* magazine named her one of the Top 10 College Presidents in the U.S., and, in 2014, she was recognized by *Fortune* magazine as one of the World's 50 Greatest Leaders.

Dr. Esther S. Gergen was born and raised in El Paso, Texas to two Mexican native parents who migrated to the United States. She attended a public high school as a first-generation American and went on to become a first-generation recipient of bachelor's, master's and doctoral degrees. Following a successful career in large corporations, Gergen was offered a full-time faculty position with the department of Leadership Studies at Our Lady of the Lake University, where she currently serves as department chair for the San Antonio, Rio Grande Valley and Houston campuses. She has conducted leadership development trainings for several non-profit, corporate, and community organizations, served as an executive member on the board for the West San Antonio Chamber of Commerce.

Cynthia Halliday was born in Rio de Janeiro, Brazil, and is a doctoral candidate at Florida International University. Her research on leadership, social exchanges, gender and diversity, and cross-cultural management has resulted in a number of publications and presentations at international conferences. Prior to pursuing her Ph.D., Halliday spent several years as the managing director in higher education settings and in corporate management, working for multinational organizations. She received her MBA from Brigham Young University and bachelor's degree in engineering at the Universidade Estadual de Campinas in her native country of Brazil.

Isis Lopez was born in Brownsville, Texas, and holds a bachelor's degree in communications as well as a master's degree in psychology. Her graduate research focused on positive psychology and cyberpsychology. Lopez has held professional positions in public relations, advertising, marketing, and editing in South Texas, before becoming the first Executive Director of Alumni Relations for a newly established Hispanic-serving university. She later started a position as a public information specialist for the City of Austin's Code Department, in which she educates the Austin community on local and international codes and ordinances as a preventative measure to make the city a livable place.

Camilla A. Montoya was born and raised in Sao Paulo, Brazil, and moved to the United States to attend college. Upon completing her degree, she taught English, French, Spanish and Portuguese at a language school in Brazil, after which she returned to the U.S. and started her career in higher education marketing. Following these experiences, and after having completed a master's degree in Organizational Leadership, she transitioned to a faculty position, teaching courses such as Industrial/Organizational Psychology, Cross-cultural Psychology, Research Methods, and Gender Studies.

Dr. Fawn-Amber Montoya was born and raised in Colorado. She completed her undergraduate degree in Utah, then went on to complete a master's degree and Ph.D. in History. Montoya completed a pre-doctoral fellowship in Texas before accepting a tenure-track line at Colorado State University–Pueblo. Montoya taught in the Chicano Studies program and the History department for 10 years before accepting a position as the director of University Honors.

Dr. Montoya is the author of a number of publications and has been awarded University Awards in Excellence for Service and Student Advising and Mentoring.

Damaris Santos Palmer has been creating and curating online content for over 10 years. She works as director of content and community for a media agency and enjoys having side projects whether it is blogging or helping online influencers connect with clients. Palmer was born in Brazil, moved to Chicago when she was seven years old, then returned to Brazil to complete middle school and high school. She had the privilege of attending an all-women's college in the United States, where she earned her Bachelor of Arts in Anthropology, and later received her master's degree in Social Documentation in California. She is a fierce believer in social justice, particularly immigrant worker's rights and women's rights.